I HATE SHOES

Four Dinghies, Three Sailboats, Two Fianceés and One Dream to Sail South

By

Scott 'Sailor' Keddy

For Andrew

CONTENTS

I
Disgruntled Spreadsheet Monkey

"You knew what you wanted and you fought so
hard/just to find yourself sitting in a golden cage"
- Whitest Boy Alive, *Golden Cage*

I was down below when Carla and Jon simultaneously took the Lord's name in vain. We were beating to windward (trying to make ground directly into the wind) along the southern coast of Long Island when the mainsail tore itself to shreds; three massive rips from luff to leach (front to back). I was at the navigation table trying to get our position plotted, when I popped out onto the deck, instinctively knowing what had happened. Running to the bow, uharnessed, the jib headsail came down and was lashed to the lifeline stanchions. My next stop was dousing the tattered main. We were heading in.

Fire Island Inlet was a solid 20 miles away and with the sun already setting we wouldn't arrive until well after dark. As we motored dead into the five foot waves, I wondered if I had made the right choice. The bow of *Winchelsea* was bobbing in the short, choppy swells; similarly to the money used to buy her, had it sat in my 401(k) for the decades I was destined to be a well-abiding engineer in Boston. I cracked a smile. *Winchelsea* was grateful that she had been given the chance for her bow to ride across the waves of the Atlantic, as opposed to remaining moored, while that money was being tossed around like a piece of meat on a hook by hot-shot Wall Street desk jockeys; I was more than happy to be riding those same waves with her.

The trip hadn't been easy up to this point either, with a torn jib at the start, due a gale on Block Island. From the outside, it may have appeared that we were struggling against many odds; odds that were fighting us like the current that rips through Cape Cod Canal, which I had been towed through in the past, twice actually. To the outside observer, no, it wasn't as simple and easy as rolling out of bed, onto the "T" and into a desk each morning, but I wouldn't have it any other way.

***

The madness and uncertainty that comes with a drastic, yet self-inflicted, change in life began when I was a fully employed engineer in the intellectually industrious town of Cambridge, Massachusetts. My roommate at the time was another Scott, one of my co-workers, and he became the best friend I had in the greater Boston area, especially after my girlfriend broke it off after a nearly three year relationship.

Yessir, that's where it all started; on a drab street in Cambridge, sandwiched between two of the most respected universities in the world. What it culminated in was: buying a boat, quitting an overpaid job with great benefits, going against the grain on what I had been groomed to do since birth, and turning my back on all the security and stability that I had spent my whole life building towards. And no, as you'll find out, it wasn't an easy decision.

Scott crashed into my life in the fall of 2008. He had just graduated from UMass Amherst and was looking for a cheap place to stay which was close to work. Lucky for us, my apartment met his needs swimmingly. It was a mere $465 per month and exactly three blocks from the office where we worked. His desk was on the seventh floor, and he was doing environmental remediation work, usually in the field, testing systems, and fixing pipes and pumps. Jealousy is a good way to describe how I felt. He would come back in the evening, after being out all day in the sun and wind, and whatever else nasty, fickle old New England decided to throw at him, and exuded the pleasure of a good day. A satisfying, hands on, justification for being alive, kind of day.

Meanwhile, my limited time on this great Earth was spent sitting in a rolling chair in a climate controlled office. I'd get home, my eyes glassy and bloodshot from staring at computer screens for well over eight hours, after having ridiculously inane small talk with people I couldn't care less about, and all I'd want to do was talk to him about the field work he was doing. Turning valves, taking samples, testing equipment; it was what I saw on paper in real, physical form.

What Scott was doing was much closer to what I had thought of when the idea of being an "engineer" was pitched to me as an adolescent. Had I known that engineering would be sitting behind computers all day, on the verge of weeping blood as a mindless spreadsheet monkey, I would have chosen a career path more wisely.

To compound matters of dissatisfaction with

my career, the middle management at the firm were not exactly inspirational people. Most were overweight. They have had the same commute for decades with the only change being that they now drove an Audi instead of a Honda. Was that really supposed to be what I was looking forward to? Is that why I was sacrificing my one and only youth? To drive a better car along the same shitty commute?

One man stands out in particular. I was working on a "high profile" international project with him and his management style consisted of beating your confidence into submission until you snapped. How he made it past human resources is beyond me. This stout, impish creature would creep around the office floor, barely perceptible over the relatively high walls of the cubicle farm. Once he found you, he would stand in the entryway of your stall, breathing heavily, and harass you with a demeaning question as to why you were doing something *your* way and not *his* way. This was about when a twitch in my thumb developed that persisted even after I left the firm.

Growing up, my dad was in the sales part of engineering. He worked for a company that sold industrial products in the municipal market. On the weekends and in his spare time though, he would create and invent products and gadgets. While other dads were out golfing all weekend, he was in the garage, or outside building, or testing, his latest creation.

In high school, I realized that my talents and appreciation for math and science were leading me towards a career in engineering and thought that was exactly what I wanted to do. I studied environmental engineering at the University of Florida and after five glorious years of undergraduate education I headed up to Boston to start putting all this knowledge from college into practice. The new career was going well at first, and I felt like a real big-shot having a desk job in a major city and all that high-brow stuff. I put my best foot forward with that career and, most of the time, it showed.

What wasn't on my radar was how political the whole game of finding work within the office was. I was basically treated like an independent contractor and had to seek out projects through the project manager. The trouble was that my engineering skills didn't translate to playing that old office game. I didn't like to golf. I didn't grow up in the greater Boston area - and wasn't on the soccer team when I was younger with one of the executive's son. I was (unapologetically) a sun-drenched kid from the south who'd rather be surfing or sailing, or on a long bike ride on a Friday afternoon, than waiting until five rolled around to head down to the pub.

In the summer, there is always a lot to do in Boston. Sailing, cycling, running, the list goes on. In the winter, however, the sun is set and gone by the time you leave the office. It's also deathly cold outside. Most of my coworkers went to the gym then, so I joined too.

Throughout high school and college, my freshman 15 stayed at bay, through outdoors activities like crew, surfing, running, ultimate Frisbee, roshambo (not the most physical, however I was on the collegiate team) but what New Englanders' considered "fitness" in a cold climate horrified me. After sitting and staring at a screen for eight hours at a time behind a desk, your typical northern office worker will head to the basement of another office building to stare at *more* screens for another few hours while on a treadmill.

I will never forget my first day in the cardio room at that basement gym, where I witnessed dozens of young urban professionals running on what might as well have been dozens of wheels in a cage, all staring down with headphones in their ears, with the same expressions on their faces as when they were sitting at their desks. After running in place for a while, they headed back to their apartments (really just larger cubicles) to stare at yet another screen or two before they close their eyes and repeat the following day. They spend their lives floating from one box to another, staring at screens the whole time. I think it's totally possible to live in one of the most populated areas of the country and not talk to anyone for days at a time.

No, can't say I had a ton in common with those people, and to socialize with them outside of the office or socialize with them period, was more than I had bargained for.

"No, Bob, I really don't care about how you spent your weekend tearing out insulation or how great your kid is at T-ball. Can I please just make my copies and get on with my day?" I managed to get the company to pay for my Master's degree and after three years of taking classes online at night that was under my belt too. By that time though, my patience with the firm was really wearing thin.

I was also lonely my first year there. I was still dating Elizabeth, a girl I had met in undergrad and with whom I had my first sailing experience. I was in my fifth year of undergrad when I took an interest in sailing, more or less on a whim. The University owned a lake off campus, and they had a fleet of Lasers. I learned how to rig them up and one afternoon Elizabeth and I went out for my first sail - complete with forgetting to put the drain plug in. Halfway across the lake a gust flipped us and sent me into the drink. Elizabeth, having experience on these boats, did the right thing and stayed dry on the gunnel.

"S-s-step on t-t-the c-c-centerboard," I chattered. The water was freezing.

I continued sailing after moving to Boston and purchased a membership at Community Boating on the Charles River. Sailing every chance I got between the months of May and October with the backdrop of Beacon Hill and Back Bay was therapeutic. I was able to build up my sailing skills at an extremely low cost and was fully confident to sail between the Longfellow to the Mass Ave Bridges by mid summer that first season.

Nine months after moving to Boston, Elizabeth came up and landed a job at the same firm. She also happened to be on the same floor, in the same department, and with the same boss as myself. One year later, we had broken it off. I can't say that she was totally to blame though; I was at a lousy spot in my life.

I had no idea how completely depressed I could get just based on the facts that it was oppressively cold outside, and I didn't see the sun for weeks at a time. Go figure. It was agony to leave the office at five from the months of November through March with no daylight to greet you; it would be *pitch black,* outside. Then, throw in the many weekends when it was just grey and rainy. Boston is home of the low-pressure system. My skin was pasty and pale, and I was gaining weight. I was drinking too much. I just felt terrible.

The break up came in January of 2009, a few months after Scott had moved in. Incidentally, he had also cut it off with his long term girlfriend only a few months before. Needless to say, that next spring and summer were some of the best times in Boston I'd ever had. Scott and I were wolves among lambs, if you will; two young and attractive professionals in an urban area with a different college on almost every block. Once the weather warmed up, we went sailing every chance we had. I bought a membership to Courageous Sailing, a local sailing club right on the harbor, and took full advantage of its privileges: which included being next to one of the most popular waterfront bars in town. I had not been in a better place, mentally, since before I had moved to Boston.

Scott was laid off in June of 2009. It still stands out vividly in my memory and was a defining moment during my time in Boston. The economy was tanking and the municipal engineering market was no exception. That same morning the guy in the stall next to me had been let go too. Off to the glue factory, I suppose. I got a text from Scott at about 2:30 that afternoon saying he had been suddenly informed of their decision, after being lured into a conference room where he was then given about 20 minutes to pack his stuff and be out of the building. This was a Friday afternoon. According to studies, it is far less likely that there will be an "incident" if a layoff is performed on a Friday. I finished up what I was working on and headed home to meet him.

When I got to our place, he already had a beer cracked and was on the phone with his mother. After he hung up, I didn't say anything in the form of condolences, I just asked him if he wanted to go sailing. Boston harbor was only a 20 minute bike ride away, over I-93 and through Charlestown. It was a gorgeous day. On the way over, I was following Scott and trying to imagine what he was thinking. He actually didn't seem too upset about it, just as carefree as ever.

After we got to Courageous, we rigged up one of the many Rhodes 19s they had, and we were soon out in the harbor with the picturesque backdrop of downtown Boston in the late afternoon sun. I started asking him all kinds of questions like: what his next move might be, if he was leaving the Boston area, if he was going to stay with engineering...but I soon shut my mouth and realized that he didn't really want to give it much thought at the moment.

If it were I who had been laid off, my mind would be conjuring dreadful, panic-ridden thoughts immediately. At least, the person I was then would have. My mind would have been in a million places at once. I wouldn't have been able to go sailing or even hold a conversation. I would have been consumed by my own thoughts and worries. Scott, on the other hand, didn't seem to have much of a care in the world and was more concerned with just enjoying a Friday afternoon on the harbor with his sailing buddy. Being laid off was beyond his control and there wasn't a whole lot he could do about it at the moment, better to just enjoy the day.

This was the first time I starting thinking that way too. Scott being laid off started my mind, and eventually body and spirit followed, down a path I didn't ever think I would take. I was raised, educated, and groomed to be a desk-driving engineer. What happened that afternoon in Cambridge changed that mindset forever.

II
Push Comes To Shove

"Slave drivers damn you 'cause you won't dig their coal/and the slaves they all resent you, 'cause you haven't sold your soul"
- Gill Landry, *Never Coming Here Again*

The bliss of a great living situation, during a carefree summer in Boston, came to an abrupt end in the later part of July when my knee broke. A case of mistaken identity and an over-zealous concert bouncer. I was laid up for eight weeks in the middle of the summer. Some serious thinking came as a result of so much down time. Scott was on a cross-country road trip with his soon-to-be fiancée Jeanine, and I was sitting on a couch in an empty apartment in Cambridge.

One of my good friends Anna visited from New York to see me and take care of some other business in Boston, but most importantly she brought me a book called *Sailing Alone Around the World* by Captain Joshua Slocum. I read it cover to cover over a couple of days (between Percocets and YouTube sessions of *Trailer Park Boys*) and was completely transformed. Of course, I had read of people doing circumnavigations before, but had always thought that was something left to hardcore adventurers in large yachts. Someone like Richard Branson comes to mind, or the Volvo Ocean 70s that race around the globe every few years, or maybe the super wealthy with a crew of 22 on a 120' megayacht. I had no idea this lifestyle of leisure, and sailing for long distances, was something that started over a century ago, coincidentally in the city I now lived in (Captain Slocum had outfitted his vessel *Spray* only a few miles north of Boston and completed his circumnavigation in Newport, RI).

Doing some internet research led me to many, many people who call this their lifestyle, even in this day and age. The gears in my head started spinning around the central idea of leaving all I know, and definitely do *not* love in New England, behind to sail all day, every day, to exotic, far-flung ports; the same exotic ports that Slocum had visited over a century ago. Little did he know but he was paving a long, blue road for an entire subculture to follow.

I started the next step by going to the library and getting a few more books. A few meant a stack as high as the bed I was nearly confined to. I read Hal Roth and his aptly titled book, *How to Sail Around the World*, volumes by the Pardey Couple and a host of others about the outfitting, lifestyle, and seamanship of becoming a world cruiser.

Shortly after Scott returned from his road trip, he moved out of our apartment in Cambridge and into one with Jeanine in Brookline, a 30-something minute trip away. What replaced him, as well as an Asian man we literally spoke 10 words to our entire time there, were three of the most despicable roommates one could have asked for. Immediately, the house and all of its contents were divided up into theirs and mine. The fridge, the dishes, pots, pans, utensils, it was all privatized.

Of course, I was still good friends with Scott, Jeanine, and a score of other people I had met during my time in Cambridge and, naturally, had them over for dinner and drinks every week or so. This, according to the iron fist of the new roommates, was completely unacceptable. While we were in the kitchen talking, laughing (and they were invited to join), they would persistently shush us from the living room because they couldn't hear *Dancing with the Stars* over our revelry. It was a shock and such stark contrast to the bliss that living there had been only months previous; with the temperatures dropping and winter approaching, I started to shut down emotionally again, but this time I recognized what was happening.

In addition, by the time I was back in the office and fully recovered, the amount of work available had started to decline, due to both the economy and because that infernal international project was finally wrapping up. When I asked my boss about any work coming down the pipeline, he solemnly said there wasn't much of anything, and that it was necessary to find work week by week, picking up scraps of projects where possible. The only projects available were similar to when I was an intern there three years prior. He said Elizabeth had a lot on her plate and that I could go ask her for some work. My sharp gaze back, said that would never be an option.

Between my living and work situations and the cold oppression of winter just around the corner, something had to give. I needed a way out, a big change.

With so many things around me deteriorating, going through the motions for another winter in New England was not an option.

The silver lining of having less work to do around the office was that it left me a lot of free time to keep researching this fascinating life of freedom. They had stuck me on a "project" that entailed copying field data from an Excel spreadsheet to a preformatted Word document. I was allowed to bill eight hours for this, but it only took four. I came in at 10, would take a two hour lunch from noon until two and leave at four. Did I feel bad? Absolutely not, that's the price you pay when you give an engineer with four years' experience some monkey intern bullshit. How in the hell was I supposed to get my Professional Engineering license with trivial busy work like that? However, the economic downturn that had left me nearly out of work had other effects, like causing the prices of sailboats to plummet. With the New England sailing season of 2009 dead and gone, people couldn't get rid of their boats fast enough, mainly so they wouldn't have to pay storage fees for the winter.

During October and November, I scoured the internet and called yacht brokers to find a deal on something in my price range that was also seaworthy enough to sail down to Florida and beyond. I looked at boats as far north as Maine and all the way down to New York. All had some kind of major flaw though, and I realized that I did not want anything with hull or deck issues. An engine that needed work, a sail inventory that wasn't totally complete, or problems with any other auxiliary system on a boat were issues I could handle, but I did not want to start doing major hull or deck work. Being seaworthy enough to get it to Boston was another requirement.

Finally, in late November, I saw an ad for a 1971 Columbia 34 in Rhode Island. After some research, I found out that the exact same make and model that had completed a circumnavigation in the mid-1990s by a guy in his 30s. The owner's asking price was $7,200, which was a little more than my budget, but given the value of one of these in prime condition; there was a chance that it could be a bargain.

I went after work the next day to see her and brought a small rubber mallet with me to test the hull and decks for soft spots. I rented a Zipcar and made my way to Warwick. She was on the hard in a boatyard, which was filled with others wrapped in plastic for their winter hibernation.

As her present owner and I climbed the ladder up to her cockpit, I looked up the mast while stepping over her transom. I was very intimidated. I had experience on J/22s before, but nothing of this size. This was large even for what I was looking for. My ideal size was 32 feet at the most, but she was a solid 34' with a 10' beam and five and a half foot draft; a little on the deeper side, but manageable for the Keys and Bahamas where you are advised to keep it under six feet if you want to see any of the far flung, remote beaches and islands.

I did my mallet testing (which, I'll admit, was more for show than substance) and was looking over the rest of the rigging as the owner told me his story with her. He had purchased her from a boatyard three years ago and had lived aboard for two of those. However, he had since got involved with a woman less tolerant of the liveaboard lifestyle.

Her ten foot beam and five foot freeboard left a lot of room below deck, with over seven feet of headroom aft and just about six feet going forward. The V-berth was huge, and storage space was ample as well. The major issue I had read about online was with the keel bolts, which on this boat were not replaced but added to, in duplicate, less than two years prior. The standing rigging was sound, as well as all the running rigging. The big X-factor was going to be the engine though, an original Palmer P-60 gasoline engine from 1972. It was actually a marinized International Harvester tractor engine.

Towards the end of our conversation, as we were descending the ladder, he mentioned that it was going to cost him $1200 to simply keep it where it was for the winter and that he'd take $6000 for it.

What was this? He was talking himself *down*?

I played it cool though, and said I'd get back to him in a day or two. On my way back to Boston that night, I called Anna and thanked her for the book; it had officially changed my life. The next morning I called the owner back and offered $5,500. He agreed. I wired the money to him the day after and just like that; I had my new home. I had a place to call my own, on the water, away from the awful roommates, and one step closer to the life I had been reading about for months and dreaming about for much longer than that.

III
Freedom

"The dreams of youth grow dim where they lie caked with dust on the shelves of patience. Before we know it, the tomb is sealed."
- Sterling Hayden, Wanderer

Maria came into my life just as I was starting to look into a boat to purchase in October. I had met her online as more and more people, especially in urban areas, are doing these days. Almost every time we met up I had something new to tell her about an article or book I had read pertaining to the cruising lifestyle, or another boat I was considering. She was instrumental in this heavy transition period of my life, and I wonder if I could have done it without her. She was a great listener and gave solid, logical advice. But she never got in the way of my dream or tried to change the path I was on, even if it meant leaving a well-paying job with benefits in the middle of an economic recession.

I had already decided on the name of my new vessel before I had even purchased her: *Winchelsea*. The name has personal historical significance as it was the name of the ship that Alexander Kady came over on in 1749. His name was changed to Kedy when he landed in Halifax (he was a member of the founding party) and then it evolved to Keddy when Clifford Keddy came to Boston around 1900. The original *Winchelsea* was a 24 gun sixth-rate frigate. She was built in 1740, captured by the French in 1758 and retaken two weeks later. She was broken up in 1761.

Coinciding with the purchase of my new boat, I started a blog. Maria designed and set it up for me, and I filled it with all of my thoughts, challenges, and day-to-day happenings as I transitioned from a job and home on terra firma to one of the more aquatic variety. The first entry was the boat going into the water, and I've kept it up ever since. Writing is therapeutic for me; it lets me vent, lash out, and speak my mind without harming those around me.

One Friday night, I was telling Scott and our good friend Alex, a six foot five brute of a man with a wicked sense of humor and an acute taste for fine cheese, about how I had actually bought the boat I was speaking of a week earlier. They were thrilled and de-manded to be members of the delivery crew from War-wick back to Boston. I started calling local marinas and found one right downtown next to the New England Aquarium with a reasonable fee for the whole season. The dockmaster/owner even gave me the name of a guy, Steve, who could help me sail it around. I met with Steve in a pub, and we discussed our plan of action. We found a weather window two days ahead, between a couple of early December gales that would give us enough time to get back to Boston.

Two short days later Alex, Scott, Maria, Steve and I departed by train for Warwick. Steve had brought some basic safety equipment: flares, whistles, a harness, an EPIRB, and a handheld VHF. There was a great ner-vous excitement on that train ride, as we knew (or, at least we thought we knew) of the adventure we were in for. We knew it was going to be bitterly cold and that our weather window was short, but still present, after double checking the forecast. On the trip down Steve and I went over places to anchor along the way if it got to be too much to handle, due to either the cold or the choppy six foot wind swell that was expected.

Although we had departed Boston very early that morning, we didn't get underway in Warwick until just after three that afternoon; we had to make sure we had enough fuel with multiple Jerry can runs and made some last minute trips to some local grocery stores. It was bright and clear as we made our way out into Narragansett Bay, and Maria started playing some random tunes on a harmonica she had found.

It was cold though, damn cold. The salty bay water was actually frozen in the harbor that morning where *Winchelsea* was docked. For warmth, I had a full under layer, pants, a long-sleeve shirt, sweatshirt, snowboard pants and jacket, two hats, a neoprene neck/face guard, two pairs of gloves, and two pairs of socks under a pair of waterproof boots. I was warm… for now.

As mentioned before, it gets dark before you leave work at five in New England from November through March, and the sun was already very low when we departed. It had completely vanished by the time we reached the Newport Bridge. At this point, we hadn't even raised the mainsail yet; we had done all this in four hours of motoring. Just as fate would have it though, the engine quit as we approached the bridge. Mainsail up!

The wind was out of the west, which put us on a

beam reach heading south out of Narragansett Bay and into Rhode Island Sound. That is where things got pretty nasty. We were no longer in the wind shadow of Jamestown, the large island community west of Newport. The only thing separating us from the strong westerly wind was, well, nothing. All that wind was piping for a hundred miles, unabated; down Long Island sound and sweeping the waves up with it until they both came into contact with the starboard side of *Winchelsea*. Every ten seconds a six to eight foot wave would come along and tip us another ten to 15 degrees to port after already heeling considerably from the periodical gusts of 20 to 25 knots.

Did I mention it was cold? Well, it was far, far colder now. The right side of my face wanted to peel away from my body. I was having a great time of it though; I had mentally prepared myself for this experience. I knew it was going to be like this. I'm not sure how I knew though; I had never been in conditions like this before.

Every time I got nervous, I would tell myself that this is what this is boat is designed for and that there really was no danger. Steve, who had a large sailing background up and down the east coast, as well as some extended time in Asia, wasn't nervous at all. The rest of the crew, Scott, Alex and Maria, weren't doing as well. Alex had already tossed cookies port-side. I had the helm at this point and thought a song would do the trick, so I burst into the theme to Gilligan's Island. No response. Thankfully, we had to jibe soon and head east down Buzzards Bay with the wind and seas to our backs.

That dropped the apparent wind to almost nothing, and eased the rocking by taking the seas that were once on our beam over to our stern.

Scott had the helm for most of this leg of the trip. While Scott and Steve surfed down the following waves, Maria, Alex and I tried to get some rest to relieve them a little later. It was nearly impossible to sleep though; it was just too cold, even with all the layers. Looking at the record the day after, it was 15 degrees that night, and with a 20 knot breeze, that brought the wind chill to about -4. Cold. Damn cold.

I went out on deck and asked Steve a barrage of questions about navigating at night. He taught me about using buoys, how to recognize their flashing patterns, how to watch for other ships, and how to tell whether or not you were on a collision course. When we could see the bridge that marked the entrance to the Cape Cod Canal, we decided to start the engine. Or, rather, Steve said it would be a good idea to start the engine. It took us another four or so hours to get to the entrance to the canal which brought us to at about 3 am.

Of course, about a third of the way through the canal, the engine crapped out again. Scott, Alex and I desperately tried to get it started again as we drifted with the strong, four knot current. Sailing is not allowed in the canal; the Army Corps of Engineers oversee all traffic that goes through and tracks boats by radar.

At about 3:30, we made the distress call that we were drifting through the canal and needed assistance. Within 20 minutes a large tug came alongside and gave us a tow the rest of the way through. They wanted to take us back to the Maritime Institute near the mouth to Buzzard's Bay where we had come from, but we insisted that they take us the rest of the way through the canal along our original route. Once through, they brought us a couple of miles into Cape Cod Bay, and we tossed their lines back to them. The wind had died to hardly a breath at this point, but there was enough for the main and genoa to catch, so we started on our way north up the coast of Massachusetts to Boston. It was almost 5:00 am.

The sun rose shortly thereafter, and Maria was playing the harmonica again. She had just got it and wasn't very good, but that was completely fine with everyone on board. We were making about four knots on a calm bay, and even though it was still absolutely frigid, Alex was up and making bacon. That boy has a thirst for bacon that knows no limits. By two, that afternoon, we had rounded the Boston Headlight lighthouse and were making our way into the harbor in a light rain. We had tried to get the engine started again but couldn't (as it turned out, running that old, marinized International Harvester tractor engine consumes a pretty hefty amount of fuel; we had run out of gas) and had to dock under sail in downtown Boston. It was 4pm and my first sailing experience on *Winchelsea* was in the books. The trip had taken us 25 hours. Maria and I walked to the T station. It felt odd to be back in a city, to have arrived there by water, and on a boat that was my own. A boat that was my new home.

I got back to the apartment and fell into the armchair. What had I just done? I had sailed a boat from one part of New England to another, in the middle of December, between two gales to get out of this miserable living situation.

That thought put me to work that very night. I didn't need any furniture on a boat; that was for sure, and those large possessions went immediately on craigslist. I also didn't need most all of the other junk that I owned, and that was either given away to friends, sold on the internet, or donated to charity. It was down to the bare essentials, and the process of getting there was refreshing. I felt so alive, rejuvenated. It wasn't the phony type of rebirth that comes from a fancy new car, a baller apartment, or a weekend bender. This was something money couldn't buy, and something they couldn't take away. It was the challenge and experience of shedding all that I owned materially for something simpler, a "less is more" attitude.

I only brought basic cooking supplies with me: a pot, a pan, two plates, two bowls, two of each of forks, spoons, and knives, a few plastic cups, a couple of coffee mugs, a tea kettle, clothes, two pillows, an assortment of blankets, and some sentimental comforts like pictures and, maybe a Paddington bear I've had since birth, maybe. That was all I needed, all I wanted.

My dad drove down from Maine to help me load all the stuff into his pickup and take it from Cambridge to my slip in Boston (all of my worldly possessions only filled the back of the cab). He was in admiration of my new direction in life. I'm glad I had his blessing, as not many other people had the same sentiments. People around the office were starting to think I was losing it. My mother thought it was a terrible idea. Then again, anything that goes against that perfect picture she had for my brother and I is a terrible idea, despite what might actually make us happy.

I still had my desk job, and the commute was longer. I no longer lived within walking distance and had to take two trains to get to work in the morning. This did not help my productivity. By that time, the international project had wrapped up, thank the good Lord, and I no longer had to deal with the buttwipe of a project manager. On the flip side, as I previously mentioned, I was stuck doing menial tasks that an intern should have been doing. I knew I had to get out of this work situation and find something that suited me. I asked, repeatedly (and well before I bought *Winchelsea*), for an inter-company transfer to a Florida office, or to a position with more time in the field; but my requests fell on deaf ears. March of 2010 would mark my three years with the company, and I would be allowed to keep all 100% of the profit sharing deposits they had made into my 401(k). Then, I decided, would be when I made my exit.

A week or so after I returned to Boston, I decided to have a renaming ceremony of my vessel from the *Windfall II* to the *Winchelsea*. It is, in fact, very bad luck to simply rename a boat but, if you follow the correct procedure, it can be done without pissing off Poseidon.

Basically, the way it works is, Poseidon has a huge list of all the ships that are allowed to sail on His surface. He keeps this list down at the bottom of the ocean in his Court. If He sees a boat sailing along He does not recognize, He'll do pretty much whatever He can to take it down. So this ceremony asks Him (politely) to remove the name of the old vessel from His list and to replace it with the new name. Then you have to give Him libations (bubbly).

The renaming incantations go something like this:

Oh, mighty and great ruler of the seas and oceans, to whom all ships and we who venture upon your vast domain are required to pay homage, I implore you in your graciousness to expunge for all time from your records and recollection the name Windfall II which has ceased to be an entity in your kingdom. As proof thereof, we submit this ingot bearing her name to be corrupted through your powers and forever be purged from the sea. In grateful acknowledgment of your munificence and dispensation, we offer these libations to your majesty and your court.

Oh mighty and great ruler of the seas and oceans, to whom all ships and we who venture upon your vast domain are required to pay homage, I implore you in your graciousness to take unto your records and recollection this worthy vessel, hereafter, and for all time known as Winchelsea, guarding her with your mighty arm and trident and ensuring her of safe and rapid passage throughout her journeys within your realm.

In appreciation of your munificence, dispensation, and in honor of your greatness, we offer these libations to your majesty and your court.

And then, to appease the Gods of the Cardinal Wind Directions, you have to say something along these lines:

Oh, mighty rulers of the winds, through whose power our frail vessels traverse the wild and faceless deep, we implore you to grant this worthy vessel Winchelsea the benefits and pleasures of your bounty, ensuring us of your gentle ministration according to our needs. Great Boreas, exalted ruler of the North Wind, grant us permission to use your mighty powers in the pursuit of our lawful endeavors, ever sparing us the overwhelming scourge of your frigid breath. Great Zephyrus, exalted ruler of the West Wind, grant us permission to use your mighty powers in the pursuit of our lawful endeavors, ever sparing us the overwhelming scourge of your wild breath. Great Eurus, exalted ruler of the East Wind, grant us permission to use your mighty powers in the pursuit of our lawful endeavors, ever sparing us the overwhelming scourge of your mighty breath. Great Notus, exalted ruler of the South Wind, grant us permission to use your mighty powers in the pursuit of our lawful endeavors, ever sparing us the overwhelming scourge of your scalding breath.

IV
Winter Aboard A Boat

"There's nothing—absolutely nothing—half so much
worth doing as messing about in boats."
- Kenneth Grahame, *The Wind In The Willows*

Again this was Boston, in the middle of winter. It got
pretty damn cold, and I only had two 1500 watt space
heaters to help keep me warm. These worked well, as
long as the outside temperature was above 25 degrees.
Below that, and they did me just as much good sitting at
the bottom of the harbor. This is where electric blankets, and a girlfriend with heat included in her rent,
came in very handy. On the relatively balmy nights, ver-
sus freezing, I slept in the v-berth near the bow of the
boat. My bedding consisted of a thick foam cushion, and
a sleeping bag sandwiched between two electric blankets with two thick comforters stacked on top. This actually kept me very warm. The trouble came when I
had to get up in the morning for work. It took all the
willpower I had to remove those layers, and they had to
be ripped off like a Band-Aid, all in one quick motion
without thinking about it.

It dropped down to a deathly four degrees for a
couple of nights that winter, and I remember waking up
on one of those mornings to see my breath frozen in little droplets, clinging to the underside of the deck above
my head. One morning, when I tried to depart
Winchelsea for work I discovered that I was frozen in

altogether. It had been right around 32 as it rained all day once in late January. During the night, the temperature dropped, and all that water froze into solid ice. The sliding companionway hatch was frozen shut! No amount of pushing, pulling, or banging could get it loose. My only choice was to escape out of the forward hatch over the v-berth and, even from the outside; I could not budge the entrance to the companionway. By the time, I returned from work my small yacht had thawed herself out, and I could use the regular companionway to enter the boat.

Another trial came in mid-February. As I stepped down from my warm, layered v-berth one morning, about half an inch of near-freezing slush met my bare toes. This may not sound like a lot, but it covered a large area and included about 3 inches below the cabin sole into the bilge area. Water was spilling in from the cockpit, and every time the boat pitched or rolled, another large gulp of water would wash into the cabin. It had rained heavily throughout the night, and with the cockpit drain clogged with slushy ice, the water had no other place to go but down the companionway to cause me some grief. After spending 30 minutes or so, in rain that was only slightly above freezing, unclogging my cockpit drain, I turned my attention to the water that had made its way into my home.

I went to the electrical control panel and flipped the switch for the bilge pump. Nothing. Flipped it again. Nothing still. I checked the batteries next, and they were fully charged. The damp feeling on my forehead that I noticed next was either due to the water fully soaking through the hood of my jacket or a cold sweat breaking out. I knew troubleshooting this thing in 34 degree rain would not be what I consider a good time. I grabbed my screwdriver and dove into the electrical panel. After removing the face, I unscrewed the wires from the back of the switch and scraped some of the corrosion off of the terminals. I touched the two wires together, said a little prayer (okay, a large prayer), closed my eyes, and WHIZZZZ...the pump came on.

In late January, a gale came through and brought 50 knot winds with it. According to NOAA, there were 25 foot waves in Massachusetts Bay, just outside of Boston Harbor, as a low-pressure system came around and parked itself over Boston. I left work and went back to *Winchelsea* at lunch time and made sure all the dock lines were secure, the bilge was pumped out, and that everything looked in order.

When I returned later, the winds were very, very strong. Boats were bouncing around the marina, and the waves looked to be about 1-2 feet, even after being dissipated by the outer docks. The winds were supposed to increase until about midnight. I went below and started watching a movie and having a little night cap. Around 11:30 I noticed things started getting a little rollier, and I could hear the wind whistling in the standing rigging louder than I ever had before. I went up top to have a look around. It had stopped raining, but the harbor was a complete mess. The waves were a solid four to six feet outside of the marina, and the outer docks and wharf did little or nothing to stop them from coming in. The massive steel docks, on the outer edge of the marina, looked like strands of spaghetti in a pot of vigorously boiling water. The wooden docks that the *Winchelsea,* and other boats around me were on, were impossible to walk on. It was all a sight to see. High tide had come in and coupled with an east wind; Long Wharf was almost completely submerged.

A dock line is a small price to pay for a lesson in chafe. I took a look around the boat the next morning, and although all of the dock lines were still in place and holding me in my slip, the bow line had seriously chafed on the chock and probably would have parted sometime soon, allowing my boat to slam into the one to my port...not good! I pulled the frayed part higher towards the cleat, got another line and tied them both off. I was thankful; having to replace a dock line is a much cheaper lesson than causing damage to another boat!

It was always dark by the time I returned to the *Winchelsea* after work, which meant the temperature had dropped to below freezing, and there was usually a stiff wind. It had not broken 32 degrees in almost two weeks in early February, even during the day. I tried to spend as little time on board as possible, and occupied myself in the evenings by either hitting the gym (I know, but it was warm and it gave me something to do), sitting in the Starbucks in the Marriott Long Wharf lobby with my laptop for a few hours, or going to a local dive bar to watch a game, have some conversation, and slug a few cheap pints. I spent an evening on board every once in a while, and I keep myself occupied with learning the different systems of the boat. I knew this would be useful when it finally warmed up.

My day-to-day living on a boat was turning into a continuous adventure. Even cooking became a new challenge, because when everything aboard is frozen solid, cooking takes a little getting used to. In order to prepare a meal on *Winchelsea* in the winter in Boston, I had to rip open one of the frozen water bottles I had in the galley, chip away a few large chunks of ice, and throw them into the tea kettle. Just after they had melted, I would rehydrate some TVP (textured vegetable protein; it's a soy-based dried protein with a long shelf life and is good fodder aboard sailboats for long trips when refrigeration may not be available), and I usually used some vinegar (which was still liquid) to add some flavor. I would then use the remaining water for coffee or tea to have with dinner. As far as vegetables go, they had to be purchased fresh on my way home from work, usually a potato, an onion and a vegetable of color. While the TVP was rehydrating, I would light the other burner, with my small cast-iron skillet on top, and put the small bottle of olive oil I had on its side in the pan. The oil was completely frozen solid, but after a few minutes I could get a few drops out, enough to cook the vegetables. I then added the TVP, added some spices, and dinner was served!

It sounds like a miserable time and more trouble than it was worth, but it was really not all that bad. I kept the boat clean, it was well lit, and I had a stereo to keep me entertained. I also really enjoyed learning about all the different systems on *Winchelsea* (i.e. navigation, electrical, water, wastewater, fuel, etc.);

I enjoyed this much more than plopping down in front of a television in an apartment.

Carefully placing the name on her transom
Photo: Maria Lobikin

V
The Journey That Changed it All

"No good decision was ever made in a swivel chair."
- General George S. Patton, Jr.

After returning from the Taint (a name I affectionately gave to An Tain, a dive bar a few blocks from my dock with dollar drafts) late one Saturday night in early April, I got a Facebook message that more or less changed my life forever. It's funny to think about those turning points in retrospect. Just when you truly least expect it, something comes down from out of the blue, lands in your lap, and sets you on a completely different course in life. A friend from college, Katrina, had messaged me to ask if I would like to join her sister and her husband on a schooner they ran on a delivery up the east coast. I almost fell out of my bunk.

I called Katrina the next day, got her sister's number and was on the phone with Seychelle that afternoon. She told me the boat was the schooner *When and If* and that I should look it up online. Their plan was to sail out of West Palm the next weekend and, with good winds and seas, be in Vineyard Haven a week or so after that. I said I was game, trying to hide the boyish enthusiasm in my voice. Typing "schooner When and If" into Google revealed that it was an 80' gaff-rigged schooner built in the late 1930's for General George Patton. He sailed on it for two seasons before going to war in Germany, and had named it *When and If* because, when and if he returned from the war he planned to sail it around the world. Unfortunately, as the story goes, he did not return.

I flew to Florida on Easter Sunday to have a cookout with my mom and brother, hung around with them for a couple of days, and went to West Palm on Tuesday morning to start the trip up the east coast on *When and If*. That's where things stopped being normal and started to get ludicrously awesome in a hurry.

Mid morning, I arrived at Rybovich Marina, one of the largest and most well-known megayacht marinas in the world, and called Seychelles. She said Emyl would be by to pick me up in just a few minutes. I walked down to the end of the dock at the marina and waited. As I looked around, I saw what I would later find out was the largest single-masted yacht on the globe, the Mirabella V. It looked like a skyscraper; it was hard to imagine a sail that large coming out of that tower. Emyl arrived, and I hopped in the dinghy. We took an immediate U-turn, and stopped by a beautiful new boat that he said belonged to a captain he knew who had just gotten in from New Zealand. As it turns out, it was the boat of Senator John Kerry, who also happened to be on board. He came over to the side, dressed as a quintessential northerner visiting the south, was decked in flowery board shorts and pink Polo shirt. Mr. Kerry shook Emyl's hand and asked if he was headed back to Vineyard Haven with *When and If*. Emyl replied affirmatively, and off we went.

Just outside of the marina, on the hook, was *When and If*. She looked very majestic next to the other boats at the anchorage; definitely a head-turner to anyone who passed by. Music was playing as we approached, and I threw my travel gear and sleeping bags onto the deck. I climbed aboard and was instantly delighted as to what I saw. I had some apprehension before this trip; I did not know what to expect of how the ship was run. I thought it would be relatively loose and casual, and I'm happy to say I was right. Tools were all over the deck, as Emyl was making some final repairs. The sails were not on yet and lay in bags covering most of the foredeck.

Emyl did not waste any time showing me around the boat, instead he headed straight forward and climbed out onto the bowsprit. He uttered something about standing there and handing him tools, and I was glad to help in any way possible. We then started putting on sails. This was a bit different than a regular 30' to 40' sloop, these sails were thicker, larger, and consequently much heavier than what I was used to. There were six sails in total: the mainsail, foresail, staysail, jib, flying jib and fisherman. The foresail was gaff-rigged, and I could not wait to see it raised.

Seychelles arrived soon after, and Emyl went back to the marina to pick her up. I took this time to take my personal things below deck and have a look around. It was just as cluttered below as it was above, but no less beautiful. They both came back within a few minutes, and Seychelles had brought most all of the provisions for the trip to New England. There were many different items including: granola, lunch meats, cheeses, chicken, some canned goods, dried foods, teas, coffee, some beer, two tanks of propane, milk, jugged water, Kombucha tea (a personal favorite of Seychelles and Emyl) and a variety of vegetables.

The rest of the afternoon was spent tidying up *When and If*, taking their boat *Dutch Maid* to get fuel (which would be left at anchor in Florida), and bringing *When and If* to the dock for the night to wait for the other three crew members, top off the fuel and water tanks, put some ice in the chest, and charge up the batteries.

It was only the end of the first afternoon, and I was having the time of my life working on this spectacular boat with a couple of people who, although we had just met, I thoroughly enjoyed the company of.

The rest of the crew arrived later that first evening. They included Hugh, a lively guy at 19 who had helped the previous summer with maintenance work on *When and If*; Drew, a 28 year old boat builder; and Toby, he was 38 and had been doing crew jobs and deliveries since he was in his early 20s. There were six of us total, and four had their captain's licenses. The combined experience on this boat was huge.

My bunk was adjacent to the galley. Seychelles had recommended this one since we would be on a starboard tack for most of the trip, and it was the driest on the boat. We were off the docks by 8 the next morning and headed towards the inlet at West Palm. Just after passing through, the sails went up in a gorgeous flurry of lines and canvas. Within half an hour, we were cruising comfortably in the Gulf Stream under sail alone at just about 8 knots.

The shift rotations started immediately after we were out of the inlet. There were three watches, two people per watch, with a duration of three hours. This allowed for six hours in between the three hour watches. It ended up working out great, and the rhythm was going well. Emyl was my watch partner. The first night we had the seven to ten pm shift, followed by four to seven am. I was sound asleep as soon as my head hit the pillow, despite a lot of movement in the galley/saloon area. In what seemed like ten minutes, Emyl nudged me on his way to the stove to put on some coffee, four am had come much sooner than I had expected. We stumbled up to the cockpit where Toby and Drew were finishing up their shift. Although it was ungodly early, it was a beautiful night, and the sound of only the wind in the sails and the hull on the water complimented the breathtaking myriad of stars overhead.

Emyl and I were on watch together, and while three hours can seem like a long time, we had some great conversations, and the time flew by. We talked about current events, politics, movies, books, and countless South Park episodes. Almost everyone I knew back then went to college at some point. Some of them probably shouldn't have, and went either because their parents forced them, they didn't know what else to do with their lives, or just to slip into an alcohol-induced coma for a few years. However, on this boat I was in the minority. I was the only one who had a degree, but judging by the actions, words, and thoughts of this group; you would have never known the difference. These were intelligent, well-read, and well-spoken people who had clear goals in their minds. They were responsible, fair, hard-working, honest and good natured. I couldn't, and still can't, say the same for all of the "educated" people I know.

At some point, we jibed. I noticed a squall ahead, and we turned to avoid it. Emyl headed forward and released the preventer. "Swing her to port and duck when appropriate!" He gave me the command at a normal volume; no need to yell when the only engine is the gentle 15 knot breeze to our backs. I turned the wheel to the left, and the solid wood, 6-inch diameter boom came racing across over my head. The sun was up at this point, although the weather was turning ugly. The squall ahead was sucking in air from all around it, and the seas were getting confused. What once were long lines of four-foot waves to our backs before were turning into more of a washing machine. Peaks and troughs were building on each other as the wind shifted and started building a swell in an opposing direction.

The remainder of the day passed uneventfully with reading and shift changes. Emyl had decided we should head for Charleston since our weather window was closing fast according to the radar. It started pouring just after dark as we made our way to the entrance to Charleston Harbor. Visibility was extremely limited, and Toby was down below in the nav station shouting the next marker to look for as Emyl manned the helm. We made our way to the anchorage, and the fisherman anchor Emyl swears by, hit the muddy bottom at just about two in the morning.

I spent the next two days in Charleston cleaning the boat and doing some light maintenance work. Fate was not on my side though, as the weather looked unfavorable to get around Cape Hatteras for the foreseeable future. I was forced to return to Boston via airplane while the rest of the crew finished the delivery.

VI
The Great Escape

"The decision to flee came suddenly. Or maybe not. Maybe I'd planned it all along - subconsciously waiting for the right moment." - Hunter S. Thompson, *Fear and Loathing in Las Vegas*

Once I was back at my desk, there was a physical pain and an emptiness in the pit of my stomach I couldn't shake. I knew I had to leave this job, and I had to leave it soon. All that next week, I scoured the internet and started cold calling boats to see if they needed a hand for the upcoming season. I replied to an ad on craigslist for a schooner in Newport. The owner John called me over the weekend, and we set a time for a longer conversation the following Monday morning. That became the most pivotal Monday I'd had in my 26 years on Earth. He gave me a phone interview and a short "quiz" to make sure I knew my stuff about sailing and hired me right then and there. He wanted to meet me, so I planned to drive down to Newport that Wednesday.

I hung up the phone and slowly walked back to my desk, heart racing and trying to keep calm.

What now? John wanted me to start in two weeks.

Give my two weeks now?

Was this it, time to make my escape?

Within minutes, my phone rang again, this time it was Emyl. He wanted to fly me back down Thursday to take *When and If* all the way to Newport. This WAS it. I went into an empty cubicle next to mine (poor guy had been let go three weeks earlier), grabbed a box and starting shoveling my personal stuff into it. I glanced over my shoulder at Marina, the girl in the cube across the corridor. She looked at me nervously and cracked a half smile. I must have looked strange to her, wearing the biggest grin she had probably ever seen me sport inside of that building as I frantically packed up my cubicle. I closed the box and headed down to my boss Mike's office.

Keeping my cool composure as well I could, I told him that I would be leaving the firm. He asked if this was my two weeks' notice and I told him that nominally, it was. However, my workload was very light, and there were many things I needed to do with *Winchelsea* to prepare to sail her to Newport in two weeks, in addition to the *When and If* delivery. He then asked if I would be around for the rest of the day. It was 11:40 am at this point, and I told him no, I wanted to catch a friend who was running in the Boston Marathon and that I would be out of the office by noon. We shook hands and agreed to complete the paperwork and exit interview before I left for Newport. My next stop was the finish line of the Marathon.

On my way out, I stopped by the cube of a particularly ornery guy Chuck and asked him if he had everything under control.

"Yeah, I guess Scott, why?"

"OK, good, I'm going to go sailing for a while."

Unfortunately, taking *When and If* to Newport

was not in the cards as the winds stayed out of the north for the next two weeks. As much as I wanted to sail that boat up to New England, I knew I had a lot to do to get *Winchelsea* ready to leave Boston and live on the hook in Newport all summer.

Spring had finally sprung in Boston, and I enlisted my good friend Christian over a few pints one night. He agreed to help me sail Winchelsea to Newport via the Cape Cod canal; a direct reversal of the journey in December. We timed our weather window with starting work in the first week of May and took *Winchelsea* out for a shake-down sail around the harbor that ended with a torn genoa. Maria spent six long hours stitching it by hand to get it ready for the trip a few days later, bless her soul.

After some light provisioning and a fuel run, we were off at 0600 on a bright, early May New England morning. Our high spirits did not last long, however, as the engine died (I would later discover it was overheating) as we made our way out of the harbor. Up went the sails, just like leaving Narragansett Bay five months earlier. We were heading along, with the genoa up, at a nice five knots in a gentle but very present 10 knot breeze. Lunch was great, prepared by Maria, who had chosen to come along again. I can't stress her importance in my early days of sailing and boat ownership. She was always supportive, both mentally and physically, and still is to this day. I dare to say I wouldn't be the carefully confident sailor I am today if it weren't for her.

By two in the afternoon that day, things started to get interesting. The wind freshened to 15 to 20 knots as squalls started to pop up in our wake, to the north of us. Then they started to fill in to our west, and finally straight for where we were headed: the bottom of Cape Cod Bay where the entrance to the canal is located. Around four that afternoon a squall finally caught up with us bringing strong, shifty winds and heavy rain. We took the sails down and started to motor towards the canal entrance. If we didn't make it by 7 pm, the current would start running the opposite way of our travel, making it impossible to complete that night. At that time, we still had just over 16 nautical miles between us and the entrance; it was going to be close. Of course, the engine overheated again about an hour after starting it, up with the sails once more! The wind had tapered off and was blowing steadily from the northwest. This put us on a nice beam reach, but not enough speed to get us to the canal on time.

We dropped anchor at about 8 that evening, cooked some steak I had brought and called it a night. It had been a long day and the currents were favorable at 6:30 the following morning; I slept soundly. The alarm going off at 5 was just too early. We were about 45 minutes from the canal and, as per usual with that infernal 40 year old tractor engine; it crapped out as soon as we rounded the jetty marking the entrance. We radioed the canal control authority as we drifted through the canal, a drill I was familiar with. This time, we just so happened to be drifting by the Coast Guard station as our distress call went out, and they came by and brought us in. An hour later, the tow boat company showed up and brought us the rest of the way through the canal.

At about 9 that morning, our sails went up in Buzzards Bay, and we were off. Lunch came and went, but by about 3, the wind had shifted from the north to the west and forced us to beat to windward until after the sun set. We changed headsails multiple times, reefed and finally un-reefed the main again at about 10 that night. We were still pretty far from Newport, and our dreams of making the Cinco de Mayo parties had evaporated. I went down to flip on the navigation lights for the night-sailing, and when I checked, they weren't working. Some wires had come loose in the anchor locker, and after 20 minutes rolling around in there, I was feeling ill. I took a nap.

When I woke up it was past midnight, and I took the helm from Christian who needed some rest as well. As the outer buoy marking the entrance to Narragansett Bay came into vision, I asked Maria what our speed was and how far we were from the buoy. She said about 3 nautical miles and we were doing about 3 knots. Perfect, an hour away. About 20 minutes later I asked for the same information, as we seemed to have slowed down. We were down to two knots, and it was about two nautical miles away. Ugh, still another hour. The same thing happened when I asked about 15 minutes after that, and she replied with one and a half miles and one and a half knots. The outer buoy was mocking us, perpetually one hour away! Finally, after rounding Fort Adams, we dropped anchor in Newport Harbor at three am, another destination met without a working engine.

Maria woke me up at seven am the next morning. She had to be on the 8:30 bus back to Boston. I went outside; the fog was so dense I couldn't see land. The wind was howling. I was grateful we had made it in a few hours before this stuff set in. We climbed down the rickety ladder to *Folicle*, my 8' fiberglass dinghy which was a gift from my dad's friend Sue, compass in hand. I knew the yacht club was somewhere to the south of where we dropped anchor. Within 30 seconds of leaving Winchelsea, I realized a) the ladder was about to break itself free from the transom and sink to the harbor bottom b) the yacht club was on a huge rock, and I had no clue where to land the boat if I even found it and c) one of the oar locks was bent and rowing with one oar in this wind was an exercise in futility. Trying to get back to Winchelsea was not easy.

We started calling marinas to find a launch service. Eventually, we got ahold of someone who would pick us up at 9. On the bright side, on our way to shore, the *HMS Bounty* appeared out of the fog, gliding along and making its way out of the harbor; I will never forget that, especially considering what happened to her years later during Hurricane Sandy.

Once ashore I wasted no time and found *Aquidneck*. I met John, the owner; Green, the captain; and Josh, the other crew member. They told me to come back tomorrow at nine, and I'd start work. I spent the rest of the day cleaning *Winchelsea*.

That night, tragedy struck *Folicle*. It was extremely windy, and I was checking my bearings on three fixed points at regular intervals. They were consistent with no signs of any dragging. The dinghy had other plans and decided that she had enough of *Winchelsea* and I and ripped herself free. I still had the line and the steel ring, and I found out later the ring had ripped completely through the fiberglass. The next morning I discovered the Old Port launch service was completely unreliable and ended up arriving almost 30 minutes late for work on my first day. Luckily, that was the earliest I had to come in during that part of the season, which gave me time to use the launch service while I searched for *Folicle*. She was picked up by the aforementioned yacht club on the rock to the south, but I discovered she had a gaping hole in her transom beyond repair.

That night I bought a similar dinghy with a 3.5 horsepower two-stroke outboard. The small engine made my life infinitely easier as I could now come and go as I please, given *Winchelsea* was about a mile from the dock where I worked. Even though I was late for work my first day I explained the situation and, being a liveaboard himself, Green seemed to understand.

VII
New Life in Newport

"If a man must be obsessed by something, I suppose a
boat is as good as anything, perhaps a bit better than
most."
- E. B. White, *The Sea and the Wind that Blows*

Training started immediately with how to properly
raise and lower a gaff-rigged sail, practicing leaving and
coming back to the dock and appropriate sail trim for a
schooner with two headsails. The weather in Newport
was ideal for sailing with a steady sea breeze that filled
in daily which would last until just after sunset. There
were some mighty fine sunsets too. The crew and two
captains of the schooner all had a relatively similar
background to myself. They were all college educated,
and most had given the corporate desk jobs a try before
finding out, exactly like me, they just didn't fit that
mold. Green had the background most like mine. He
came from Florida, went to the same college my brother
attended and was an IT computer guy at a large firm
before leaving to explore the Bahamas with his then
girlfriend (soon to be wife). He ended up in Newport a
few years before I arrived where he currently lives on a
44' ketch with his wife and two daughters. A pretty
good life, in my opinion.

Some locals have told me that the spring I was
there was the best run of striped bass (called striper,
oddly enough) in decades. I went on deck one evening

after sunset to check the anchor rode, and all I could hear were huge stripers coming up to the surface to grab the squid that make their way to the surface at night. They made a huge splash and a gurgling sound as they swallowed them with a big helping of air. The next day is when I found out they were squid, and another local told me how to catch some. All I needed was a bright light and a squid jig. I took a quick trip to a tackle store and found what I needed. No squid that night though, but the light did attract a bunch of wormy things.

My coworker Josh came over, and we each had a line in with our backup frozen squid I got for $1 per pound at the fish market. We didn't catch a thing. Josh had to go back home, so I untied the dinghy. He was having trouble with his hook, and I thought I had tied the dinghy off and turned around to help him. I thought wrong. The line to the bow of the dinghy slipped into the water, and it slowly started to drift away.

"Josh! Boat hook! Now!"

He grabbed it and rushed up to the deck. I extended it and leaned overboard as it just drifted out of reach. It was drifting away FAST in the wind. He said something to the effect of this not being good and that we had to do something fast, but I was already below changing into boardshorts. I told him to get the swim ladder ready, told myself aloud to NOT think about how cold this was going to be, and dove in. Maybe it was the adrenaline, or maybe it was a sign I was becoming a little tougher since leaving a cushy desk job, but the cold didn't really affect me. I swam to the yet-to-be-named dinghy and climbed on. Later, Josh mentioned how impressed he was with my speed in that whole process: boardshorts to back on board in less than a minute. I motored back to Winchelsea; Josh climbed on, and I took him back to shore.

To give a rundown of what my new day-to-day job was, I hopped up out of my bunk at about eight every morning. This was, in all actuality, earlier than I had been getting up during my last few months at the desk job in Cambridge. I got dressed, made some oatmeal, packed a lunch and was hopping down onto my dinghy by 8:30, motoring from the anchorage near Ida Lewis to Bowen's Wharf across the harbor. Once tied up at the dinghy dock I'd head to the Seaman's Church Institute for a cup of coffee and possibly a shower if time permitted. I'll be honest; there wasn't a whole lot of showering going on that summer. Most of the time, especially when it warmed up and I was drenched with sweat after work, I would jump into the harbor with a bar of soap when I got back to *Winchelsea.*

I was on board *Aquidneck* by nine and working on the daily checklist. Our first sail, with complimentary mimosas, was at 10. It was the job of myself and the other crew member to raise and trim the sails after getting off the dock, serve some drinks and, most importantly, act as animated as possible while telling visitors everything they ever wanted to know about Newport. In all honesty, I thought we did a pretty damn good tour, especially when there was a blow on. We got that 80-foot hunk of Awl-grip coated steel humming along at nearly 10 knots a few times, roaring back into the harbor on a beam reach. There was always something special and unexpected to see too, whether it be Naval ships or a megayacht coming in, the start of a race, a music festival at Fort Adams or even tenants of Clingstone mooning us.

For most of the summer, there were five two-hour trips daily with the last one returning at about 8:15 in the evening. After cleaning up the boat, it made for a 12-hour day. It was exhilarating though, and I was extremely happy doing it. I was outside, sailing in one of the most beautiful parts of the country, talking to people on vacation. The pay wasn't bad either; I was making more on average per day than I was at the high-brow engineering firm.

As the summer went on, my knowledge on board *Aquidneck* was growing by leaps and bounds. Green and Isaac were starting to give me much more responsibility, and I was beginning to seriously consider getting my captain's license. The many different types of boats that come through Newport is amazing, and they did not hesitate to educate me on what they were, their advantages and disadvantages, historical significance, etc. I had stumbled across a very special part of the country, if not the world, given the awesome pedigree of sailing that inhabited Newport.

There is something that allures people to boat owners that I can't really describe. It's just something you have to experience. I threw some really great parties on *Winchelsea* that summer in Newport. Later in the summer, the water taxi ran all evening until nearly 1am. This allowed my fellow crew members and I to

52

hand pick certain *Aquidneck* customers to meet us out at a local watering hole later in the evenings. After a few drinks there, the late-running water taxi could whisk us all back to *Winchelsea* for an after party. By mid-summer, we had this routine down pat, and it became a stunt we would pull multiple times every week. There were times though that we would miss the water taxi, and I would have to take people back in my dinghy, making multiple trips back to shore.

I had made friends with a local musician named Matt, who played regularly at one of the places we would frequent with our new found friends. On one particular night, Matt, two ladies and myself had missed the last water taxi out to the general anchorage. Throwing in the towel not being an option, we all piled onto my dinghy; which had never been tested with four people. The thunderstorms that had threatened all evening were finally upon us, and as we clambered to get into my small boat, the rain started pouring down in torrents.

Not that the rain mattered in the least; within seconds of pushing away from the dock at King Park and pointing the dinghy towards *Winchelsea*, the bow was submerged, and the rest of the small boat quickly followed. I somehow kept a hand on the painter, as the rest of the crew tried to figure out what exactly had just happened, as well as how to get out of their current situation. My clothes and jacket were weighing me down significantly, and it was too deep to touch the bottom and stand up. I swam back to the dock, swamped dinghy in tow, and hopped out. What a scene: three bodies trying to swim back to the dock, and a huge mass of flotsam slowly drifting away. Not wanting to jump back in and struggle with clothes on, I did the only thing logical and took them all off.

As the other three survivors hoisted themselves back onto the dock I made repeated swims, totally nude, collecting the scattered debris and bringing them back. A few minutes later, my clothes were back on covering the places they should, and the dinghy was being bailed out. Multiple trips back to *Winchelsea* were the only way this endeavor would actually work, and luckily for both Matt and I, the girls thought the whole thing was hilarious. All they wanted were some dry clothes and a stiff drink to warm them up, both things I managed to provide once we were on board.

Most of the get togethers on *Winchelsea* that summer were small, simple gatherings of people that worked on the wharf, with some of their friends tagging along. I met a lot of great people that way. There were also some great raging parties that lasted all night long. One that stands out was the Fourth of July when the fireworks were set off just a few hundred yards away at Fort Adams. The harbor was warm, and we spent most of the night diving off of *Winchelsea*, playing music way too loudly among other lewd and debaucherous behavior. I also met Carla that night, a girl who would accompany me on the first legs of leaving the northeast.

There an electric energy in the air that summer. Those of us that worked seasonally in Newport knew our time was limited together and, as such, had to make the most of it. This led to a level of revelry

I hadn't experienced since my early years of college. And, through it all, I was never late nor missed a day of work. It was an interesting dynamic too. Typically, the guys sailed and crewed on the boats while the girls worked at the ticket counters, neighboring restaurants and other little shops that dotted the wharfs.

After the Fourth had come and gone, my thoughts began to drift towards what I would do at the end of the season. One thing was for certain: I would be heading south. New England winters and I get along like a raccoon and a bear trap, and I couldn't tolerate another one. I planned to leave in early to mid-October, depending on wind and waves of course. I already had one person on board for sure, a great girl Carla, who did landscaping and construction and had plans to bike across the country the following year in a custom trailer she was fabricating out of aluminum. My kinda people. I was looking for at least one more and ideally two, and by the end of the season I had convinced a coworker to join me. I imagined, that it would take me between 2 and 4 weeks to get there. I had completely made up my mind about that plan, no matter what condition the engine was in. I was heading south on *Winchelsea* in October, period.

However, my attitude towards *Winchelsea* and her ability to take me all the way south to Florida had started to change. I was working on the inboard engine and had replaced the carburetor (the old one was cracked and leaking fuel) and had solved the overheating issue by rebuilding the water pump. However, for some reason, it was still not running reliably. Sometimes it would start up in an instant and run indefinitely. On the other extreme, it could take many attempts to get it running and then die soon afterwards. There was no rhyme or reason to it. I decided to get a 15 horsepower outboard and put it on a bracket that would hang off the stern. Not the most glamorous or eye-catching option, but it would at least get me where I wanted to go (provided the water was relatively smooth). After purchasing said outboard and bracket, I discovered the dimensions wouldn't work, and the propeller would still be out of the water with the bracket all the way down. That was a lot of money and effort down the drain. It was back to the inboard, and I was taking it south no matter the condition, my mind was made up.

I honestly didn't have much of a plan for myself once I got to Florida. One option was to start getting stuff together to get my captains license. Or, I could hop on a tour boat in south Florida, the Keys, or the Caribbean like the job I had in Newport. I could simply get daily work on boats doing maintenance and repair, and the occasional delivery job while I continue sailing south through the Caribbean. I could also keep sailing through Panama and on to San Diego as originally planned. I had options.

In August, I finally got a way to charge my batteries consistently: a wind turbine. This made a huge difference. When I first came to Newport my batteries were shot, I had a small solar panel with the incorrect voltage for my batteries, and no engine/alternator combination to produce electricity. I was charging my iPhone at work and using candles at night on the boat.

It wasn't the most convenient arrangement, and it certainly needed improvements, but it worked for a while.

I first upgraded to a larger, more appropriate solar panel, and with that I could now charge my phone, turn on a couple of lights for a few hours and even use the VHF radio, wow! I also replaced the batteries for free since they were covered under their warranty. My dad generously gave me the wind turbine for Christmas since he's in the industry, but it was a long road of failed installation attempts followed by saving some money for the factory mounting kit and finding a day to do it.

I wouldn't have considered it living "green" before, simply because my needs were not being met. I was getting by, but I couldn't run my computer, or any of my sailing instruments or running lights. With the turbine now up and running, I had fully charged my batteries in only a few days of a stiff 15 to 20 knots of breeze.

All that being said, I'd say I was probably in the running for one of the greenest people out there. The only fossil fuels I used were a little propane for cooking and about a gallon of gas every week or two in my dinghy. Living that life, and working on projects like those, really showed me that you can live pretty comfortably with a lot less than you'd think. And actually, given my lifestyle, the view I woke up to every morning, my line of work, and people I've met, I'd venture to say I had a bit more.

Another story to regale is the dinghy disaster of epic proportions. The day started so very, very well. It was a Friday; Maria was coming in from Boston just before noon, and Geoff, running late as usual, was due to arrive just after 2. The plan was to take *Winchelsea* out for a spin, even though there was very little wind. I was fine with this because I had just rebuilt the water pump the week previous, and was anxious to see if that really did solve my engine issue of shutting down after less than an hour of running. By 2:30 we were off of my buoyed anchor and motoring down Narragansett Bay.

After over an hour, the engine was still running smoothly, with no changes in RPMs or sounds of her struggling. We had been motoring up wind, so we could have a nice down-wind run coming home. It was a picturesque Friday afternoon in August sailing on Rhode Island Sound. On the way back, the wind died, but we didn't care; we had no place special to be. I flipped the engine back on as we approached Fort Adams and rounded the point back to my makeshift mooring. Geoff and Maria picked it up from the bow and tied the boat off; couldn't have been simpler.

After enjoying a couple of beers, we heard a shout from across the water. My neighbor Matt was calling to us to share a bottle of wine he had just opened. I had not met him before, but the boat had been there for a couple of months now. I use the term "boat" loosely here. I should say yacht, proper yacht. I should really say absolutely gorgeous Swan 56. He had been captain of this yacht for about a year. He was 30, from North Carolina and had taken a similar track that I was currently on. After some good conversation and wine, we went ashore to meet up with some schooner people.

Just after midnight, Maria, Matt and I went back

to our boats. Maria and I dropped Matt off on the Swan, *Perseverance*, and headed towards *Winchelsea*. I was helping Maria on board, standing on the aft bench in the dinghy. Maria couldn't quite get herself up, came crashing back down, and fell back a bit towards where I was standing. At this point, things went from peachy to disastrous in a hurry.

Within seconds, and I do mean literally seconds, the stern was submerged. Within another two the bow followed it and in another three my dear dinghy was on her way straight to the bottom of Newport Harbor. I felt below me and dove down in the pitch black water, desperately thinking that there may be some neutral buoyancy in the hull, but to no avail. At this point, my thoughts turned to getting myself out of the harbor and trying to collect the flotsam that was now drifting away with the wind and current. To my left, I heard a motor running, and it was Matt in his dinghy (although I guess you'd call it a tender, I don't know) to the rescue. He plucked Maria and I out of the harbor, and helped us retrieve the jerrycan, oars, and fender. After I was back on *Winchelsea*, I went to sleep. Oh, my iPhone was in my pocket too; awesome.

I took the water taxi into work the next morning. I told Isaac about my mishap, and he advised to recover it. As long as the engine wasn't running, he reasoned, it would be just fine. That night, it was a Saturday in mid-August in Newport, and the town was jumping. I wanted to join my friends who were going out, but I instead went over to Green's boat and borrowed his dinghy for the night. Back on *Winchelsea*, I tied my cast iron skillet to about 25 feet of line and spent the next two hours dunking it up and down as I drifted with the wind, "feeling" for my submerged boat. I came across what I thought might be it twice, noted the location and set the watch I borrowed from Kevin for 6 am, sunrise. I woke up the next day to yet another wind shift, which meant I had to start the search over. Back into Green's dinghy with the skillet, I again plucked around for an hour trying to find it, which I thought I eventually did. The only issue was that the tide had come in, and it was a big one due to the proximity of the full moon. To my best estimate, my dinghy was now in about 25 to 28 feet of murky water. Oh, and it had just started to rain. I went back to *Winchelsea*, put on fins and a mask and attempted a couple of free dives.

Now I'm sure with good visibility and some practice this would have been a walk in the park, but I was not afforded either of those. Instead, I blindly dove where I thought it might have been and didn't even make it to the bottom. I must have been close though because it felt like I was really, really deep. I decided this was a vain attempt and had to call someone who had some scuba gear. Luckily, Josh did. To add to our luck, we both had the day off Sunday so we could attempt the recovery. In the pouring rain, with winds upwards of 25 knots, and visibility of about 2 feet, Josh managed to locate the sunken dinghy. Within 10 minutes we dragged it to the surface and in another 20 Green had come over and managed to nearly rebuild my little 3.5 horsepower two-stroke. Again, I never stop learning from these great people I've met. It took me another two days to get the engine started again, but I got her running! I had decided to rename the dinghy *Phoenix*.

Another trial of living on a boat followed soon after the dinghy disaster. I had a doctor's appointment on a Monday in late August at about noon in Boston. A massive low-pressure system had moved over New England starting Sunday morning. It brought a ton of rain and winds in excess of 35 knots. Green had mentioned this on Sunday as we struggled to surface my dinghy, but I didn't think too much of it since my anchors had shone through a gale in mid-May with winds that hit 50 knots.

I left Newport on Monday morning bound for Boston. After the doctor appointment, I went to the library to use a computer and read a bit. It was a little weird, because at just about 4:30 pm I was reading <u>Sailing to the Reefs</u> by Bernard Moitessier and the chapter was about these massive gales that rip through Cape Town with winds over 80 knots. He was telling about how well his CQR anchor holds, and my thoughts happened to drift to *Winchelsea* and how she was holding up in this small gale here. Well, had I not forgotten my iPhone on my boat, I would have had a new one by at this point, as the library was adjacent to the Apple store in Boston. I would have received Green's call, as well as the ones from the harbormaster. At about 6:15, I met up with Elizabeth, and we cancelled our plans for a Red Sox game and decided instead on a movie. Elizabeth, yes the same one that sent my life into a tailspin a year and a half ago, was back in my life. We had rekindled something when she came to Newport with her family a few weeks prior and had made plans to see each other in Boston. I asked to use her phone to check my messages, I still had that feeling. And boy was that feeling correct.

Green had left a frantic sounding message at 4:19 telling me *Winchelsea* had "broken free" and was dragging anchor through the mooring field to the south. That was what did it: the wind direction. My anchors were set to the prevailing winds in the area which came from the southwest. Even strong winds from the east and west would have been alright, but 35 knots from the north were definitely troubling. I called Green and he said it was holding where it was for now (which I later discovered was because my anchor rode had wrapped itself around a lobster trap) but if the wind shifted I would be bumping into lots of boats. He also said there wasn't a lot I could do tonight, but had to take care of it first thing in the morning.

Sadly, I told Elizabeth we'd have to postpone and that I had to get back to Newport as soon as possible. She gave me a sweetly devilish smile and said that was too bad, she was hoping she wouldn't have to go home alone that night (!). Why, of all the possible nights for *Winchelsea* to drag anchor, did it have to be this one? The next bus didn't leave for two hours and would get me into Newport at 10:30. We had some dinner, and I tried not to let it bother me too much. There wasn't a whole lot I could do at this point, and these are the reasons why I had as much insurance as I did.

Once I returned into Newport, I had to really

convince the water taxi driver to take me out to that part of the harbor. When we got out there, I could see why. I had never seen waves and wind like this in the harbor before, but from talking with Green it was nothing unusual, especially as fall comes. I found *Winchelsea*, hopped on board and checked out the anchor situation. I still had both; they had simply dragged. Taking Green's advice (again), I headed to bed and waited for the morning when this was supposed to calm down.

When I woke up, I hopped out on deck to see if anything had changed. Not much had. I was in the same place, but it was blowing a lot less fiercely. Also, the harbormaster was just showing up to greet me. She asked why I hadn't answered my phone, and I explained the situation. I gave her Green's phone number and asked her to call it since I needed a pair of warm hands driving *Winchelsea* in order to get the anchors up. Green showed up about an hour later, and he manned the helm as I pulled the chains and lines aboard. The amount of sea life that had grown on these lines was considerable, and they were slippery as hell. I eventually got it all up, and he set out to a place in the harbor that was a little more protected. I dropped them there, and that was at about noon.

Looking back, it could have been a lot worse. That lobster trap may not have been there, and I could have been pushed back further into the mooring field. If this had happened two weeks earlier, my engine would still be in pieces all over my cabin, and I wouldn't have had any insurance. And, most importantly, what if I didn't have friends like Green, Josh, Geoff and Maria? I don't even want to think about it.

Sailing aboard Aquidneck

VIII
Preparing for Points South

"Go small, go simple, go now."
- Larry Pardey, *Cruising in Seraffyn*

In the first week of September, Hurricane Earl threatened to bring 100+ mph winds across Newport. I had a few options: stay in Newport harbor at anchor, follow Green up the bay to a protected cove, or get her hauled out of the water. A mooring was not one of them because Oldport Marine, who owns most of them in Newport, kicks people off when there is a hurricane watch or warning; go figure. I decided to get her hauled out because my insurance would pay for 50% of the cost, plus she desperately needed to get her bottom painted before we headed south where all sorts of sea creatures like to grow in the warm water.

The "hurricane" ended up being a mild gale by the time it hit the Northeast, but better safe than sorry, thinking back to my previous experience with gales. I took her up on a Thursday morning and got her back 8 days later. I did the trip up single-handed, from raising the anchor to docking, and the engine worked like a dream the entire way. On the way back Matt joined me; it was a great day for a boat ride. I spent the week staying at various friends' places on land in Newport and working. It was a nice change, but by the end of it, I was ready to go back to being gently rocked to sleep, snug the in the V-berth.

With all of that behind me, I had just a hair over three weeks left before I wanted to head south. I was looking at a ton of different routes, planning how much time it would take me overall, thinking about all the stuff that could go wrong....and it did nothing but freak me out. I talked to people about it, and they agreed that both my boat and myself were ready for the trip, but it was still pretty daunting. I simply couldn't think of it as one long trip down south that would probably take me over a month. If I did, I started to get overwhelmed, doubt myself and start thinking crazy things like selling *Winchelsea* and moving back in with Mom. I had never attempted a journey this great before, especially with myself as captain, and I was apprehensive. I had to think of it in little steps, small coastal cruising trips that I could handle.

Like all good things that must someday end, summer in Newport was coming to a close. We said goodbye to a fellow crew member bound for law school in mid-September, and another left to finish college a few days after that. There was a definite nip in the air, especially at night. Fall was approaching; there was no mistake about it. I planned to leave sometime during the second week of October. The tourism would significantly slow down by then, hurricane season would be nearly over, and the cold fronts would (hopefully) not have moved in yet, bringing fierce winds with them.

My general plan was to head out of Narragansett Bay, hook a right and go west into Long Island Sound. Then it's down through Hell Gate, the East River and out into the Atlantic. I'd probably stay outside of the ICW as I pass by New Jersey, duck in around Cape May, and sail up Delaware Bay and then down the Chesapeake. From there, I'd stay inside around Cape Hatteras (I'm bold, but not that bold) and after Beaufort, NC stay mostly outside with a planned stop in Charleston. From there, I'd make a B-line for Jacksonville. I'd probably stay there for a few days, and if the timing is right, catch the Florida vs. Georgia football game around Halloween. I'd then make my leisurely way down the coast of Florida, around the Keys and up to Sarasota, *Winchelsea's* home port that she's never seen before.

I planned to stay within 25 miles of shore the entire time, which was the limit of my TowBoatUS membership. I was also well insured, for liability and loss of the boat, so I really had nothing to lose. When it was all said and done, I estimated it would take three to four weeks to get to the Florida border. I had been saving money for the trip, but I figured it shouldn't cost a whole lot.

Our planned departure date was October 4th. The crew being Jon, a guy who worked on the schooner next door, myself, Carla and of course *Winchelsea*. Three weeks prior to sailing, I had an absolutely massive checklist, which I had whittled down to only getting the proper paper charts a few days before we departed. I purchased an EPIRB, a harness to clip anyone working on the bow into the boat and a spotlight. I patched a hole in the exhaust, installed the depth sounder, fixed the chart plotter/autohelm, as well as taken her on a couple of shakedown sails, among a galaxy of other tasks that don't come to mind right now. During our sails, we discovered she really loves an early reef, and in 15 to 20 knots of breeze there was only a small trace of weather helm. I would have liked to get a new mainsail, the current one was sufficient but a little stretched out and baggy, but her sail plan called for a 13 foot, when most modern rigged boats have a shorter one in the 10 foot range. Oh well, maybe in Florida.

I really couldn't wait to get south of the Mason-Dixon line again. Warmer, milder weather (it was already getting too cold for me in Newport by then), my family and friends were all waiting for me. We planned to stop in Charleston and Savannah for a few days at least; Jon had yet to truly experience southern belles and their hospitality. Of course, we were in no rush; trying to sail on a schedule is how you get into trouble. However, I wanted to be south of Hatteras as soon as possible. Again, there was no crucial urgency, but I had a certain personal reason I met in Newport that summer who was waiting for me to get to West Palm sooner than later.

A few days before departure, all the prep work was complete. *Winchelsea*, Jon and I, with Carla, were ready to go. The checklist I made nearly a month previously had exactly zero items left without a strike through, and all that remained was a little bit of organizing, weighing anchor, raising sail and following a compass heading. I decided to move our departure up a bit, from early on the 4th to the afternoon of the 3rd. I had also changed the route; we would sail on the south side of Long Island and bypass the sound. This would put us well within a good weather window for the nearly 40 hour sail to New Jersey, and allow us passage through the heaviest shipping lanes out of New York during daylight hours; a win-win. It was still a few days off though, which means it could change drastically, so I was keeping a close eye on it.

I was really going to miss Newport overall. It had been my introduction to the sailing community, and I had felt welcome from the get go. Green and Isaac had taught me so much, and Green had been more than helpful on numerous occasions. From my carburetor, to the wind turbine, to my water pump, salvaging a dinghy from the bottom of Newport harbor, hurricane preparations, and pretty much any and all advice I could have ever asked for; he is the closest thing I've ever had to an actual mentor. I was practically begging for something like that at the engineering firm, and they never delivered. I learned about 12 meters, weather watching, currents and tides, to watch out for erratically moving boats, etc. It's hard to put words to it, but I felt 1,000 times more solid in my seamanship than I did even 6 months prior; it's a feeling of confidence you carry with you. Anywho, I felt ready to take the next step and give myself a real challenge sailing *Winchelsea* south. To draw an analogy, it felt like I'd been building a roller coaster. The chain had been pulling me up to the first summit. The tension was mounting as I reach this peak. I was about to go over the crest. It was just me now, coasting....I just hope I've laid out enough track below as the ride begins...

IX
The Journey Begins

"And you, you will come too, young brother; for the days pass, and never return, and the South still waits for you." - Kenneth Grahame, *The Wind in the Willows*

We left Newport at about 0800 Sunday, October 3rd. It was chilly, but the winds were a nice 10-15 knots and in a favorable direction. Sails were raised just outside of Fort Adams, and away we went. Once out in the sound, the seas were a moderate three to five feet with an occasional six to seven foot anomaly. We jibed around Point Judith, where the seas increased slightly, and the wind started to pick up. I knew there was a gale warning for that night, but it looked like it would be here a little early. At about 11 am I made the decision that we would put into Block Island for the night instead of pushing for Montauk.

By the time we were within sight of the channel into the Great Salt Pond at Block Island, the wind was gusting to 30 knots. As we approached, I rounded up into the wind to lower the sails. I'm not exactly sure how it happened, but I looked up at that point to see a huge rip in the jib, and the leech cord (now free from the actual sail) wrapped around one of the spreader lights. A quick flick of the wrist, with the knife out of my pocket, took care of that, and the sail came down. The sail, unfortunately, was damaged well beyond repair. The main came down without incident.

Once we were in the anchorage area, I decided to grab a mooring instead of anchor as the gale passed through. I didn't think it would be an issue, considering 90% of the moorings didn't have boats on them. We tied up, cleaned the decks and cockpit and took a nap. Later that afternoon, I woke up to radio the harbormaster about our situation, and ask if he knew of anyone with a jib they were looking to unload. He got back to me an hour later, with a negative on the jib, and also to inform me that the mooring would be $20 per night! Thanks for the hospitality and rubbing some salt into my freshly mangled jib. I'd understand if it was peak season in mid-July, but it was a gale in October. I'd bet dollars to donuts he pocketed the cash. Sheesh.

There was a tiny weather window on Tuesday afternoon that could get us to Montauk. The wind was supposed to calm, although only slightly, and remain in a favorable direction until it clocked around to the west that evening. The only problem was the sea state, which was still around eight feet with a very short period. Not a comfortable ride at all. Considering that, combined with the fact that going to Montauk will only save us 10 miles on our trip to Cape May, I made the decision to forgo getting the crap beaten out of us for a very small return. I ordered a new jib from Florida and decided to wait this thing out until Friday. I really couldn't believe how hard it was honking with gusts over 30 knots out of the north from Sunday through Tuesday. Wednesday and Thursday it did the same from the west. It was November weather in October. High pressure was supposed to build in from Canada that weekend, which looked like a good window to shoot straight from Block Island to New Jersey. In the meantime, Jon was making a chain of Monkey's Fists and Carla was knitting a headband. I attempted to make a bag out of the destroyed jib, but my hand sewing skills needed lots of work.

The jib came in on Thursday afternoon, and we thankfully left Block Island on Thursday evening. The seas had calmed, and the wind had shifted into a favorable direction so, just after sunset, we left. Montauk light was soon abaft as well, and the stars were the only lights we could see on that moonless Thursday night. Jon and I took hourly shifts at the helm and Carla kept us company and awake. And Mountain Dew, lots of Mountain Dew. And cigarettes. Massive amounts of tobacco. Bursting out into a caffeine and nicotine induced version of the Gilligan's Island theme song at 3 am was reminiscent of the trip from Warwick to Boston 10 months earlier.

Just after sunrise, the winds shifted. They were starting to build out of the west, and we were quickly beating into a 25 knot headwind. Sailing close hauled in those kinds of conditions makes for the most strain you can put on a boat, from the crew to the rigging to the sails. In comparison though, the stress from the wind was mild compared to working at a desk job six months before. I thought about all that had happened so far and that, finally, I was leaving New England. Departing from Block Island the day before was my farewell to that region and the winter that was to follow.

As the sun started to fall low, in the direction we

were trying to make progress, I went below to check our position. I had turned on the GPS and was plotting the coordinates on the paper chart I had bought second hand when the mainsail burst. John and Carla were taken by surprise, but for some reason, I knew that was about to happen. It was ripped in three places, from the luff clear to the leech. I can't explain why but right before I went below I could almost physically feel the strain on the sail from sailing this hard. I should have let off and run south, towards Cape May. It was a moot point, I thought, as I scrambled to the foredeck to get the jib down. I went back to the mast to release the main halyard as John fired up the old Palmer to get us into Fire Island Inlet, the closest harbor, about 20 miles to our northwest. We were lucky though; there are not many places to put in on the southern shore of Long Island.

Normally, I try and avoid coming into an anchorage at night, but this was an exception. It took us five hours of pounding into five foot chop to reach the inlet. The sun had set long ago, and with the flashing red lights of radio towers in the background, the light pollution from New York City, cars on the seaside highway and boats coming and going, I could not make heads or tails as to where the channel was. There are nasty shoals that come out from the two offset points of land which force a vessel into an elongated S-shaped course. The markers and buoys are not plotted on the chart because they change so frequently. John and Carla were up on the foredeck trying to get the attention of passersby as we did doughnuts where we knew there

74

was safe water.

"Where is the channel?!" John yelled to an incoming fishing boat that dared get close enough.

"You're in the channel!" they replied. We decided to follow them in, and I think they got the idea because they slowed down considerably.

However, the amount of shoals and lack of lit buoys eventually caught up with us and landed *Winchelsea* in about four feet of water, and she draws five and a half. A call to a tow company got us off, and we asked to be brought to a marina. The next morning, we found and reinforced the spare main, which happened to be the original sail from 1971. I was hoping, praying that the 40 year old dacron would get us all the way to New Jersey, when I could get another sent up from Florida.

Fire Island was a great place. The people were some of the friendliest I've met, and I really enjoyed Columbus Day weekend there. It's a tourist town, strictly seasonal, as are most of the residents. The restaurants, bars and shops were all closing that Monday, so it was a great time to visit. The little village of Ocean Beach was more or less deserted, outside of a handful of locals and a few tourists trying to pretend like the summer wasn't quite yet over. We got to know these locals, the people who stay there year round, and they were fascinated with our story of leaving our lives behind to sail south on a 40 year old sailboat and that the only reason we were there was exactly due to fate and our mainsail ripping some 20 miles from the inlet. They did a lot for us: showed us how to navigate the bay without running aground; where the best places for fuel, food, music and booze were; giving us local specials on drinks (since it was pretty much just us and them); and even offering us a ride to the mainland for a couple of supplies.

We were docked in Lonelyville and the only way to get to Ocean Beach was to walk a couple of miles along the beach. I did a lot of thinking on those daily walks since there wasn't a whole lot else to do while we waited for more favorable weather. I still could hardly believe I was actually doing this, and that it was working out, despite some small setbacks. But, I reasoned, this was all part of it, part of the adventure, the chaos, the thrills and the chills.

The only trouble we ran into was right before we left. When we were towed into the marina after running aground, the tow boat operator said that it was out of season, and that we could stay here for free. *Winchelsea* was one of six boats out of what seemed to be 100 slips. We stayed there for four days, and as we were about to untie our lines a couple of guys came up and asked if we wanted to "settle up". I gave them a look that expressed both confusion, as well as annoyance, and asked what exactly they meant by that. They said I owed them $77 per day for each of the four days I had been there.

I did not get angry. I did not lose my cool. I calmly said, "Well boys, this is the first I've heard of it, and the guy who towed us in said it was out of season and there would be no charge."

They replied (and I'm paraphrasing here, they

were of the type that struggles with logical thoughts and sentence structure simultaneously), "we're sorry, but you have been misinformed. And, surely, you must have seen us collecting from other people all weekend."

To which I rebutted, "so you knew I was here for four days and you are just getting around to me now? This boat basin doesn't look that busy! I had no idea what you guys were doing, selling ice cream and raffle tickets for all I know or care, but if I knew it was going to be $77 per day I'd have pulled out and anchored the second I was towed in!"

They said something about how that didn't matter, and they I still owed them $77 * 4, which I refused to actually multiply for the sake of my own blood pressure. I could tell at this point that reasoning was just not going to work with these fellas. I told them that I only have about $50 cash on me, knowing there was not an ATM for miles. They said they only take credit cards and checks.

"Well guys, I'm truly sorry, but you are out of luck. I don't have a lick of credit to my name, nor a checking account. I'm living free and clean of all that nonsense. I can send you a check in the mail when I get to New Jersey though, if that suits you." They agreed, and a phony name and address later, we were off the dock.

Jon and I, just the two of us, departed Fire Island, New York on the following morning, a Tuesday. It was October 12th. Carla had left the previous day to visit friends in the City and get back to Rhode Island for work. The wind was calm, a steady five to 10 knots as we motored out of the inlet and completely died shortly thereafter. The engine on *Winchelsea* again performed like a champ and powered us towards Barnegat, NJ for 8 solid hours. When the sun went down, we had a steady 15 to 20 knots of wind out of the north on our backs and a following sea. Life was good. It was a bit of a struggle to keep her from crash jibing as the weather helm would push us one way and surfing down a wave would push us another, but from hour to hour, shift change to shift change, we got the hang of it.

More tobacco was consumed, mirroring the night from Block Island past Montauk. It keeps you warm, in both body and spirit. We were back on hour shifts, which left about 45 minutes of rest after plotting our position and finding a spot to lie down. Then *Winchelsea* wanted to talk and keep you from getting any real sleep. The steering cables and pulleys squeaked and talked to us; John can confirm. In a high-pitched voice, she would ask us where we were going, what we were doing, among other things our tired minds would make up from the rhythmic, almost human tone the steering system produced. Atlantic City was visible a long ways off, which we passed by in the wee hours of the morning. I wondered who might still be up in that crazy town, and if they might be looking out at the ocean, watching a small blue sailboat with white sails pass silently by.

By sunup, we were within 15 miles of Cape May! We had ripped through the night at an average speed of over six knots. By 10am we were motoring into the inlet and dropped anchor 15 minutes after that. I ordered a mainsail from a used sail dealer in Annapolis. However, that was not without trouble. I called literally a dozen marinas around the Cape May basin, and nobody would do me the small favor of accepting a UPS package. I finally persuaded a guy who ran a marine supply shop to help me out, and he admitted, "they don't take kindly to sailors around here, sailors never spend a dime when they pass through." Even when we arrived to pick it up, he half joked about selling it to us since it was now his property. Well, I'm sorry if I have to spend money to achieve a basic level of human decency. It would have been no trouble to accept a package, I even explained that my sail had ripped on the way here, really hammed it up sob story style. Thanks but no thanks, New Jersey, I can't get out of here fast enough. It's sad but true; people there are only nice to you if you have something to give to them, and that something is cold, hard cash. It's like they have some sort of complex about being so close to New York that they feel the need to stand out, but at the same time secretly wish they were New Yorkers.

We had to sit patiently through yet another gale as we waited for the "gently used" main from an Irwin 34 to come in from Annapolis and after four days we were headed south of the Mason Dixon. It was Sunday, October 17th.

We left at the crack of dawn, bound for Norfolk. I really couldn't wait to be in the south again, after over three years in the north. I know I was excited to move away up to Boston when I graduated college, but it's just so much more...fun, down there. Surfing, sailing, biking, the beach, long days in the sun, beautiful warm nights and it's all year long. Sure, it gets a little steamy for a bit in the summer, but it's a small price to pay.

Our original plan was to head towards Virginia and the mouth of the Chesapeake and to keep going south to Oregon Inlet, some 30 miles north of Cape Hatteras and head inside there to Pamlico Sound. Being a responsible mariner, I called the local TowBoat US guys down there to see what the conditions were like at the inlet. Unfortunately, he said he strongly recommended we do NOT try and go through Oregon Inlet; it has severe shoaling and a really powerful current. He said he didn't want to tell us flat out not to, but if he had a 34' sailboat with only a 22 horsepower engine, he'd go the ICW route from Norfolk instead. So that was our new plan. It is 100 miles of straight motoring from Norfolk until we could again set sail in Pamlico Sound. That's 18 hours. Two nine hour days of Winchelsea using nothing but her engine in a narrow man-made channel, her 39 year old gasoline powered tractor engine that had given me a fair share of trouble in the past. I was pretty sure I'd worked out all the issues she had over the past summer, outside of completely rebuilding it, but this would be quite a test.

Jon and I then sailed from Cape May outside around Maryland and came into Norfolk late Monday afternoon, after nearly 40 hours of travel on *Winchelsea*. Her engine, I have to say, was an absolute champ. We ran her for a total of 17 hours on our trip from Cape May. The first instance was leaving the harbor and putting the sails up. After sailing close hauled over flat seas for six or so hours, they started to build and the wind shifted to a direction that was exactly where we were looking to head. Not to tempt fate again by beating into a 20-25 knot headwind in 4-6 foot seas, I decided to turn on the engine and motor. We only made about 4 knots, but *Winchelsea* took the seas with ease. I checked the weather, and the winds were supposed to calm and shift around midnight, which they did. Then it died completely.

Since I had a massive hole in my exhaust, it was impossible to sleep in the cabin while the engine was running for fear of affixation. Even though there was next to no wind, we decided to keep the engine off and get some sleep even though we weren't really making much headway. It was a beautiful night though; the moon set around four in the morning, leaving only the stars out. There was not even another ship in sight, only radio towers winking softly on shore in the distance to starboard. During my four to five AM shift, I turned out the bright stern light and enjoyed the view above me, and the bioluminescence *Winchelsea* made as she sailed slowly through the night under a full main with the jib just barely filled. I even was able to set the sails correctly and put on the wheel brake, thus allowing her to sail herself, balanced perfectly between the two sails and the slightly offset rudder. I laid back and put my feet up. This was what I had been searching for.

The sun rose just after seven and by eight, we were motoring again, following the rhumb line to the mouth of the Chesapeake. Motoring in was uneventful, outside of the bottlenose dolphins and pelicans we saw!

Ah...truly back in the south. It was a wonderful 75 degrees with sunshine and a huge blue dome overhead. Around noon, I changed into shorts. One year prior, in this same week, I was driving through Connecticut back to Boston and it actually started snowing. This week in 2010 could not be more different.

Monday night, when we got into Norfolk, we had the pleasure of eating with an Admiral in the Coast Guard, Jim Watson, the father of Elizabeth, my girlfriend from Boston and college. He's one of the most personable, down to Earth guys I know and gave Jon and I some great advice for fixing up Winchelsea, a bit. The hole in the exhaust was in a section of 2" steel pipe, and I thought the only solution would be to weld it, or have it replaced entirely, which would be expensive. He said he had a similar problem on his own boat and replaced it with a length of high-temperature hose. Jon and I spent over three hours the next morning cutting that piece of pipe out with a hacksaw and the afternoon finding that replacement hose. It worked fantastically. We also got the alternator working again, so despite the fact the wind turbine was completely shot (I think something happened to it during our first gale at Block Island), we could charge our batteries without having to pay for a marina slip with shore power!

After those repairs, we left Norfolk Wednesday morning and spent four days on the Intracoastal Waterway. Easy as pie. If you passed Kindergarten, you can navigate the ICW. All you really need to know is the difference between red and green (or triangles from squares), stay between the lines and, if you get confused, follow the leader. It was my birthday during that leg, so we more or less drank the boat dry one night and blared a classic rock station on the radio at anchor in the middle of a cypress swamp. A pretty good way to ring in year number 27.

Jon and I arrived at Beaufort, NC on Friday afternoon. I decided to take a break for a couple days, enjoy this great southern weather, and see a friend as she passed through. Our plan at that point was to make either Charleston, SC or Jacksonville, FL by Halloween. The warm weather and friendly people in the south were really starting to make this trip very enjoyable.

Jon and I preparing to depart Block Island
Photo: Carla Norton

X
Winchelsea Dies, the Dream Does Not

"The dream was never over/the dream has just begun" -
Fleetwood Mac, *Straight Back* (as covered by Washed
Out)

On Wednesday, October 27th, the voyage of *Winchelsea* came to a halt. Jon and I awoke that morning with the hope of continuing our journey south. Those plans were thwarted however when I pulled the dipstick out to check the oil. I was horrified; the "oil" was white and of about the same consistency of butter left on the counter overnight. Water had somehow made its way into the engine. There are about a hundred ways for this to happen, and they can range from a simple clog in the exhaust to a hole in the block of the engine itself.

Two oil changes and a $90 valve on the exhaust later, we weighed anchor and tried to motor out of Beaufort harbor. I put it into gear and pushed the throttle forward, nothing. I ran below to check that the carburetor was opening, and the cable was intact, they were both fine. Back to the helm to try the throttle again...nothing. This was serious. The engine was starting to stall, and it just sounded sickly. I could tell not all four cylinders were firing. I called to Jon to throw the anchor back in.

Normally, I would have dove right in to fix the problem, but this major engine issue was out of the scope of the trip. Basically what it came down to was money, time and resources. I was down to less than two grand in the bank after new sails, dockage, gas, food, beer, belts, hoses, etc., etc. I still needed to get to Florida, and I refused to throw good money after bad. The engine needed to be totally rebuilt, or replaced with a newer one. I just simply couldn't afford to continue with *Winchelsea*.

I gave 110% of myself to that trip, and it really hurt to call it quits. We were fully prepared, handled every adverse situation that had been tossed in our faces, and, up until then, emerged victorious.

As much as it broke my heart, *Winchelsea* was put up for sale. The boat that got me started on this crazy trip when I bought her nearly a year before and radically changed my life would soon belong to someone else. It was a damn shame though; her hull was in great shape, the rigging was stout, there was plenty of room below and she was completely paid for. It became a point of diminishing returns though, and she had to go. I can only hope she changes the next owner's life as much, and for the better, as she did mine.

As soon as she was sold my plan was to head to Fort Lauderdale. My personal reasons for going to West Palm were on the rocks, and the jobs to be had on boats in Lauderdale are much more promising and plentiful than West Palm anyway. I figured I'd find a regular old terra firma apartment and work doing deliveries and at a marina/boatyard.

Jon left the day after I called it quits. He was a great help, and a great friend. He was also planning on

Lauderdale, after going back to New England for his car, so I was sure I hadn't seen the last of him.

I had zero regrets about this whole thing. I learned a ton and actually, considering I didn't have to pay rent in almost a year, they weren't expensive lessons.

After getting over the initial shock of the engine completely failing, I realized I did have some other options besides to sell the boat straight away.

This was my reasoning:

Option 1: Sell the boat. I could probably get between $3,000 and $4,000 for her, considering the engine is pretty much shot. This extra cash would definitely help in rebuilding my life down in Florida.

Option 2: Transport the boat to Florida on a truck. Not a viable option at $3,000. That's like 6 months' rent.

Option 3: Diesel repower. Not an option at this time at about $8,000. Just don't have the cash.

Option 4: Keep her up here. I could just leave her at anchor, talking with the locals leads me to believe this is a viable option. I'd definitely have to keep that liability insurance though. The only trouble would be trying to sell her remotely, or if I chose to keep her, I'd have to still repower at some point, which would be $8,000 as noted above.

Option 5: Scrap. There are 4,700 lbs of lead in

the keel. Lead goes for about $1.10 per lb right now, which is over $5,000. I really don't want to do this to her though. I'd gladly take half that to keep her intact and in the water under a new owner.

Based on all these considerations I decided selling her was the best option. I planned to spend the next week or so in Beaufort trying to sell her. After that though, it may be the scrap yard.

I had quite a time living in Beaufort for a few weeks during this whole debacle. I would even go so far as to say they may have been some of the most significant I'd experienced in my entire 27 years on the planet.

The day I decided to sell *Winchelsea* that the voyage, in its present state, was over; the girl I had met in Newport called to tell me she was no longer interested in when I was getting to West Palm, and that she didn't want to see me when I did. She was kind of my emotional and physical light at the end of the tunnel, so really it was only fitting that it ended when the journey came to an abrupt halt.

I spent the next four or five days sorting out what I would take with me, what was tossed and what I would be leaving for the next owner. That was a painful process. There were times when I literally had to sit down, take some deep breaths and realize that *this* was the final destination, and there would be no glorious feeling of dropping anchor in West Palm or Sarasota. Like I had said before, I had a great run with that boat and there were no regrets, it could have turned out much worse.

After the boat sold, it would be only me. No boat, no girl, no job. Just a suitcase, a backpack, a train ticket and the entire world before me to do as I please; total and absolute freedom. My first stop in Florida would be Orlando; I sent some packages to my brother's house there where I planned to stay for a few days of decompression and surrounding myself with the familiar faces of family and old friends. And I had to buy a car. I hadn't owned a car in almost four years, and I can't exactly say I was looking forward to it. Then it's off to Fort Lauderdale to start over again.

Although that small coastal town along the ICW in rural North Carolina changed my life forever with a smattering of decidedly painful events, aside from those, that place was actually pretty terrific. The scenery is gorgeous. The general anchorage area is right between a quaint row of restaurants, bars, hotels and marinas and an island with a troop of wild horses that come to the water to drink daily, 25 yards from my boat. The inlet is right around the corner from this island, and every few days dolphins make their way into the anchorage area to feed. Not to mention the weather was just fantastic. It was nice to have some time to myself to write, reflect and line things up to get my life back in order.

The people there are equally amazing. It's a pretty small town, so in my 10 or so days that I spent there I got to know a few people, and they were all interesting characters. A couple of people who stick out in my mind are this guy Todd, who is pretty much the only cab driver in town. While I was moving my life out of my boat, I got to shore one morning with about 10 garbage bags full of belongings. I loaded them into his cab, and on the way to the Pack'n'Fax place he turned around and said "Hey, aren't you the kid who's having a rough week and is trying to sell his sailboat??" I didn't say a word; I was dumbfounded. "Yeah, man" he continued, "people were talking about you at the pub last night. Oh, and didn't your girlfriend break up with you too??" I almost died.

"Yeah, that's me. Know anyone who wants to buy a sailboat?" He said he did, actually, and that he'd give my number to a friend of his.

Another was this guy Bill. He works at the bank across the street from the dinghy dock. I walked in there the morning Jon left and asked him where the library was. Not only did he show me, he drove me there. No kidding, right in the middle of his work day. In addition, the woman at the coffee shop has been giving me free coffee all week since I've been in there on my computer almost every morning. There are a number of other fantastic people I've met here, all extremely friendly and looking to help in any way possible. A couple stands out, Jay and Lindsey, who lived aboard a tiny Grampian 26. She worked at a wine bar and Jay and I ended up hanging out there nightly. We exchanged info before I left Beaufort. It was nothing short of amazing and in stark contrast to the relative scum I had the unfortunate luck of coming across in Cape May.

I ended up selling *Winchelsea* on eBay after some leads on craigslist fell through. I got only a few hundred dollars short of what I had paid for her a year before. Considering I didn't pay rent or utilities the entire summer in Newport, I'd say I ended up on top financially.

On the morning of Friday, November 5th I left Beaufort, with *Winchelsea* in the hands of her new owners. They were a couple from Texas who flew in two days after the eBay auction ended with a cashier's check in hand. They had quite a sparkle in their eyes and a spring in their step as they made their way down the dock, a scene I am sure *Winchelsea* had seen before. I spent 45 minutes showing them their new purchase before I got into a cab bound for the airport.

They say that the two happiest days you have as a boat owner are the day you buy her and the day you sell her. It's not true though. I was sad as hell.

"Girl From the North Country" - Bob Dylan

If you're traveling in the north country fair
Where the winds hit heavy on the borderline
Remember me to one who lives there
For she was once a true love of mine.

Well, if you go when the snowflakes storm
When the rivers freeze and summer ends
Please see for me if she's wearing a coat so warm
To keep her from the howlin' winds.

Please see from me if her hair hanging down

If it curls and flows all down her breast
Please see from me if her hair hanging down
That's the way I remember her best.

Well, if you're traveling in the north country fair
Where the winds hit heavy on the borderline
Please say hello to one who lives there
She once was a true love of mine.

If you're travelin' in the north country fair
Where the winds hit heavy on the borderline
Remember me to one who lives there
She once was a true love of mine.

XI
The New New Beginning

"I cannot not sail." - E. B. White

My first stop was Orlando and bought a car during the few days I spent with my brother. It was as I had hoped and expected, relaxing and surreal to be back in Florida with friends and family. The beard that had been growing unabated since Newport was shaved clean. And, as planned, I drove down to Fort Lauderdale and checked into a crew hostel with other like-minded people in roughly the same age bracket. They were from all over the world, but many from New Zealand, Australia and South Africa. But, while they were all looking for spots on motor yachts for the upcoming Caribbean season, I was looking to stay relatively put and find some day work. I found an eccentric owner of a CSY 44, and we did an entire diesel replacement, including the two 55 gallon fuel tanks and most of the through-hull fittings.

In mid-December while playing football in a parking lot with some of the hostel roommates, tripped over my own two feet and landed on the back of my head. I went to the hospital the next day after throwing up continuously and discovered it was due to a subdural hematoma. My brain was bleeding. I decided to go back to Sarasota, where my mother lived, and was pulling out of the parking lot the next morning when I got a phone call from my cousin. His brother was in a coma after an accident on the Navy base he was working on in

Hawaii, and eight agonizing days later he passed away. This was four days before Christmas. The funeral wouldn't be until late January (he was cremated), and I never returned to Fort Lauderdale.

Instead, I spent the month of January in Sarasota with Mom, taking classes and submitting the paperwork for my captain's license. I also happened to get matched with a girl who would accompany me for the next year, Alaina. We met through a mutual friend, and the chemistry was there from day one. Like a lady, we didn't consummate that chemistry immediately that had to wait a few weeks. Her family was great too; her father had a Gulfstar 41, a solid, older cruising boat that he had just restored. We had a great few months in Florida while I worked odd jobs and prepared to head west.

In February, I helped a friend move out to San Diego. We drove an 18' moving van from Sarasota to the Golden State in three days, including a nonstop stretch from Austin to the Pacific. I stayed in San Diego for a week and bought a boat. It was a Ranger 26 called *Jazz*, just barely big enough for two people to live quite uncomfortably. My sights were set to get out to San Diego and experience the west coast so Alaina and I drove out there together in March. We took our time mostly, stopping in some of the sights along the way, trying to soak up as much Americana as we could.

Once out in San Diego we spent our first week cramped together on *Jazz*. The west coast was already showing its differences with seals and sea lions fishing around the docks every morning. The air and sea had different energies than the Atlantic; a consistent, cool stream of swells that endlessly crashed onto the cliffs and beaches, even when the wind was dead calm. Emphasis on the cool, there would frequently be a difference of 20 degrees from the sea to a few miles inland in the high desert. The water never warmed up enough to not wear a wetsuit, something I was not expecting. The seabreeze also created a marine layer that nearly prohibited beachgoing in anything, but full clothes until mid-July.

Employment wasn't too hard to find, and I got a job at a boat rental place for a smidgen above minimum wage. We shared a studio that was a converted half of a garage in the college area of San Diego, about five miles inland off of I-8, which helped keep the rent down. When I was hired, my first assignment was re-rigging an aging fleet of Catalina 22s they used for rentals. The stark difference between the yachting pedigree I had become accustomed to in Newport and the brash culture of Seaforth, a shady southern California boat rental company, became apparent almost immediately.

Having my captain's license, I tried to get on a list of available skippers for charters and regattas. I quickly found out this was not the best idea, given the condition of the boats. Another skipper had taken a Catalina 250 out (a smaller version of the 320, the 320s sailed pretty well, but the 250s were like potatoes with masts) with a full boat of 6 guests and the rudder fell off the transom across the bay. The boat drifted into a marina and caused damage to some boats, even after the skipper had thrown the anchor (there was a serious lack of rode onboard as well). The rental company turned their back on this skipper and washed their hands of it, holding him liable for damages. After hearing about this, while covered in gas filling some decrepit Bayliners with a leaky tank, I walked out the same day. I would later discover it was one of the best decisions I ever made.

Alaina had other thoughts. We had been there six weeks or so at that point, and things were rocky at best. Rent was cheap enough for San Diego (which was still exorbitant given the conditions) but between my nine dollar per hour job at the boat rental place and her only working 15 hours per week at a water store (a new concept for me, even being in the water industry for four years) money was tight at best. I also found out she had a proclivity for going from just a little upset to a total DEFCON 2, threatening to break it all off and be on the next plane home, within seconds. She was a little homesick already and had even been back once for her sister's graduation.

My good friend Matt from Newport flew in from Hawaii the next day and after a couple days in San Diego; we piled into my champagne 1988 Ford Escort hatchback and headed up I-5 to Los Angeles. He had a friend in Malibu we could stay with, and having never been up there, I jumped at the chance. This car, beater if you will, was a champ with gas mileage. The needle barely moved the entire trip. After perusing Venice beach and the taping of some sort of meat head obstacle course TV show, we drove down Santa Monica Boulevard, and I paralleled my whip directly between a classic Lotus and late model Lambo in front of the Gucci store. A proud moment for all three of us. I Googled restaurants nearby and found a Hooters. Perfect. Malibu was next, and we spent the night at his friend Kelly's place, rounded out with some libations and guitar playing.

The next morning, while Kelly was making some eggs, I checked my email and if there were any responses to my post on a cruising forum. Immediately after quitting the boat rental company, I had posted online offering my services as a delivery boat captain or crew hand for hire. I had received a response from a guy who had a Hylas 49 in Hawaii and was about to sail to Alaska. He said he had sailed with his friends from San Deigo to Tahiti and up to Hawaii the previous year and was looking for someone with more experience for this longer and possibly more treacherous journey. I replied enthusiastically, and he said he was landing at LAX in a few hours, dumbfounded by the serendipitous perfection.

I met him later that afternoon in LA, and he laid out his general plan for the trip. We would spend a week or so in Hawaii outfitting and provisioning the boat for the voyage, his friend John would meet up with us (who, he warned, had exactly zero sailing experience) and we would weigh anchor and head north as soon as the weather routing people said it looked good to go. We would aim for Sitka and spend the next few weeks along the inside passages, heading north to Glacier Bay and down to Ketchikan. I expressed interest and after a rate was set he bought my tickets on his iPad right in the hotel lobby where we met. I was to depart in two days.

I drove back to San Diego that evening and called Alaina on the way. She took it well, better than I thought. It ended up being a total of six weeks, and she got to know two of my best friends, Mat and Ed, from high school who moved out there a couple years prior. They bought a Pita Pit, a chain of restaurants popular in college areas specializing in Mediterranean style pita pocket sandwiches. Business was turbulent at best and, as typical with two novice business owners, they had little free time. I said goodbye to the three of them with an evening at the dirty Blvd Bar on El Cajon Boulevard.

XII
Terrapin Flyer

"Some rise, some fall, some climb to get to Terrapin" -
Grateful Dead, *Terrapin Station*

I got my first whiff of tropical Pacific air stepping off the plane and into the night in Honolulu, waiting for the owner Alex to pick me up. We drove to Ko Onlina Marina on the leeward side of Ohau. As we passed by Pearl Harbor, I couldn't help but think about my dear, departed cousin Andrew, who lost his life there less than six months prior.

A friend of Alex was driving us in her car, she was a resident. I stayed pretty quiet in the back seat. We got to the marina and walked down the dock to *Terrapin Flyer*, mentally pinching myself and thinking about a week earlier I was a dock lackey for a bunch of aging sail and power boats. As I stepped on board and had a look around, something was amiss. Every single flat surface on the yacht was covered with stuff. The sole, tables, counters, settees, all of it was full of food, clothes, gizmos and gadgets, water toys, fishing gear, safety equipment, engine spares, and scattered about with zero organization. While not undoable, it was shocking and instantly apparent how much work had to be done before we set out for the other non-contiguous state.

We spent a day organizing and doing some other electronic work and headed out for Kauai on the following evening. After fueling up and leaving the marina, we headed northwest across the Kauai channel.

Alex suddenly said, "And over your left shoulder, the Southern Cross."

I wasn't expecting it at all, and it hit me hard. I was surprised to see it as we were still in the northern hemisphere, and could still see Ursa Major (the North Star) off the bow. It was there though, and much brighter than I had thought. After reading about it so many times in Slocum and Moitessier books (among countless others), seeing it so dramatically and without expectation blew me away.

By dawn, the trade winds had risen to 15-20 knots out of the east/northeast. This was again something I had read all about, but had very little experience in. They weren't gusty winds like ones in the northern Atlantic and were as consistent as the swell. We anchored in Hanalei Bay at about 10 am. Alex knew some people in this area he'd like to stop in and see, as well as do our last preparations, provisioning and grab John at the airport. All of this took about 10 days; I had a great opportunity to explore the island including a hike on the famous Na Pali Coast. Waking up every morning anchored in that bay, surrounded by a full 200 degrees of beach and mountains, was breathtaking. We had a few late nights at the Tahiti Nui, one from which Alex didn't wake up until about four the next afternoon so I swam to shore and spent hours walking that beach. I didn't talk to anyone, just walked and eventually swam back to the boat.

John, Alex's friend from California who had been

at a music festival in Alabama, arrived a day before we left. He was about my age and a chef in a restaurant that specialized in southern comfort food. It was immediately apparent why he was selected for the trip, despite his lack of sailing experience. In addition to his skills in the galley, he was a great listener and storyteller. He always had something interesting to say and knew how to keep a conversation flowing. This is probably the best skill to have on a delivery, especially one as long as this would be. It doesn't matter how much someone knows about sail trim or AIS or storm tactics if they are a chore to be around it can easily double the mileage between two points.

If I had said I wasn't anxious or nervous, you should probably have been worried. I had a weird kind of giddy anticipation and with a touch of the nerves it put a knot in my stomach knowing for the next three to four weeks, I would not be within sight of land. We would actually be over 1,000 miles from any shore at some points. We got all our safety gear in order, including a life raft and survival "Gumby" suits. All in all, this boat was extremely well outfitted for the trip, not to mention the boat itself is a hulking, heavy cruising yacht that was made for these kind of passages. I had been dreaming of doing a trip like this since my first days sailing on the Lake Wauburg in college and the Charles River in Boston.

We weighed anchor a few hours before sunset on Monday, May 30th. The trade winds, those wonderful, steady and moderate breezes that blow in predictable patterns the world over were a consistent 20 or so knots.

The seas were rough, being blown by the trades unabated from the southern part of Mexico, and were strong blue rolling mounds that rose to nearly twice the height of the deck, peppered with smaller whitecaps that crashed against the hull of *Terrapin Flyer*. After the ceremonious shot of rum was poured out to Neptune below (as well as to members of the crew), the sun had set and the first round of night watches began. Alex ordered an alternating three and four hour watch regime so we would not be stuck with the same schedule each day.

The first few days were the roughest of the trip. We were sailing on a close reach against the east to northeast trades with the swell moving the boat quite a bit. Admittedly, we did not fall into our groove and get used to the motion of the boat until about 48 hours had past. On our second night out from Hawaii, I had been off my watch for two hours and was trying to sleep in my bunk, which was on the port side just forward of the mast. We were on a starboard tack, and I could feel the waves and wind (by the heel of the boat) increasing. I knew John was on watch, and he had the least amount of sailing experience between the three of us. The wind was on our starboard beam/quarter, and we were surfing down some large waves.

As we reached the bottom trough of a wave, I could feel her port rail dip and really dig into the trough as we rounded up. The autopilot would kick on and steer us back on course. However, without even getting up from my bunk I could tell that we were surfing down the waves way too fast, and the heel when the rail dug in at the trough was too much. I went up to the cockpit and saw John reading, not paying a whole lot of attention to the conditions that had deteriorated. I asked him how fast we were going. He said pretty quick, the GPS had flashed 12 knots as he answered, and we surfed down a wave. Surfing at 12 knots in a 49' boat is too fast, not to mention the rail was almost always underwater, and it took the autopilot a bit to recover. The wind had also picked up to gusts of 30 knots. We still had full sail up. John and I took in a reef and a half (roller reefing headsail and main), and she calmed down. The long waterline and heavy hull of the Hylas 49 took it like a champ, and it was actually sailing pretty comfortably.

After we passed through 30 degrees latitude, the winds calmed to a steady 20 and the seas diminished. By our fifth day, we were out of the trades and riding between a relatively weak high and correspondingly low pressure system that followed us on our now more northeasterly route. We fished, ate very well and read books like it was our job. The autopilot was on and steering the entire time, and none of us had to touch the helm on the entire trip to Alaska.

We were in daily contact with the shore via email (connected by the sat phone) and sent our position to loved ones and our weather routing consultants. Around the eighth day, we were advised to change our heading to a more easterly route to avoid a strong localized low-pressure area that was moving towards our course. We took the advice and changed course for a few days, and then started north again after it had passed. The most I learned on the trip was how to use modern communications on a sailboat and using a satellite phone to download weather information. Not difficult by any means, but just something I had not been exposed to on my experience coastal cruising the eastern seaboard.

However, the most valuable thing I took away from the whole voyage was the experience of being at sea for 17 days and getting over the anxiety of what is over (way, way over) the horizon when you're 1,000 miles from any sort of landfall. And, to be flat honest, it was no worse, and in some ways much less anxious than coastal cruising for one reason: there isn't anything to run into when you're 1,000 miles from land. As long as you keep the ocean on the outside of the boat, and the bow pointed in a very general direction towards your destination, you're all set. Avoiding storms helps out a lot too, and I'm sure I'll run into one someday, but with modern weather routing and updates via satellite phone, those can be readily avoided as well.

We sailed through the Pacific trash gyre about 800 miles north of Hawaii. I had read a lot about the phenomenon prior to the trip, and had heard various reports including a massive physical island of garbage, hazardous to marine traffic. We kept our eyes peeled and one morning I looked over the side to see some quarter-sized pieces of debris that looked like plastic. They started sparse, but increased as the day went on. The size also increased, to the point where I saw larger objects such as barnacle covered toilet seats, a whole variety of recreational balls, massive, tangled spheres of thick line that had (presumably) fallen from commercial ships, among much more unrecognizable flotsam. By the next morning it was gone, so the stretch was less than 160 or so miles. It was profound though, seeing that amount of plastic trash at least 800 miles from a remote island chain and well over 1,000 from any continental landmass.

Around the same time, we caught a dorado (mahi-mahi, dolphin, what-have-you). We had lines trailing all day, every day and brought them in at night. John pan fried it in some butter with a dash of salt and pepper. It was simple and let the flavor of the fish shine through. Outside of the fish that was caught, the only other wildlife we witnessed on the passage to Alaska were the great albatross. I probably saw five or six of them total, each larger than the last as we made our way further from land. Their wingspans can reach nearly 11 feet, and the couple that I saw, were on the upper end of that measurement. They would appear on the horizon, just a few tens of yards above the surface of the waves, with their heads always pointing down, looking for fish. They would come close to the boat, circle once or twice and then drift away on the trades, all without a single flap of their great wings.

The sun disappeared for almost the entire second week at sea, making my attempts at celestial navigation impossible. I did get some practice in the first week, although I realized quickly that I didn't bring all the required tables and books for a complete calculation of our coordinates. As we approached Alaska, the wind died, completely as the north Pacific high, a pressure system that hangs over the Gulf of Alaska for the summer, took over our weather. We ended up motoring the last three days into Sitka over a glassy, lake-like sea with trace amounts of swell. Land was sighted on the morning of June 14th, and we were tied up in Sitka by 10am, Alaska time.

It was strange walking on land again after 17 days. I couldn't wait to talk to someone else besides Alex and John, no offence to them, I just needed some variety. Sitka, like most places along the panhandle of Alaska, is a small town with a large fishing population. We visited a national park, had some much awaited beer and spent the day resting on a boat that wasn't moving. We didn't stay put for long however and were soon heading north toward Glacier Bay National Park. Three days out from Alaska, heading in from Hawaii, would be the last time I'd sail *Terrapin Flyer* for a good long time, as all of the straits and fjords that made up the inside passages were mostly too narrow to safely sail in, in addition to the lack of wind the northern Pacific high left us.

We motored up to Glacier Bay over the next two days and spent a few in the park. There are a lot of glaciers up there, hence the name, and we managed to motor ashore in the dinghy to experience a few first hand. There are some that come and meet the sea face to face with large pieces calving off into the ocean every few minutes. We got pretty close to one of these when a particularly large chunk fell within 50 yards of us. Navigating around these mini-bergs was a challenge and it required someone on the bow telling someone at the helm how many degrees port or starboard to turn to avoid a hole in the hull. It was also here I took a dip at the most northern latitude we would reach, swam over to a 'berg at least half the size of the boat, touched it and swam back. I did this stunt in board shorts, sans wetsuit. The water is an opaque milky turquoise, which I was told was from the high concentration of silt.

The next two weeks were spent making our way down the inside passages, through Juneau, down Stephens Passage, stopping in Petersburg, navigating the Wrangell Narrows and ending up in Ketchikan. We'd stop each night in some secluded, unnamed anchorage and sometimes go ashore for a hike. I'll admit I missed Alaina a lot, and I called her every time I'd get a couple bars of service out in the wilderness, which wasn't often. I called Mat once or twice and asked if they had seen much of her. He said he had, but when he asked her what she'd been up to it was something vague like scrapbooking all day, which I found hard to believe. She had said she'd be looking for another job to fill her time in, as well as her bank account. When I asked her about this, she assured me not to worry since her family was taking care of it. I wasn't sure how I felt about this at the time, I guess if my family had the same resources to support me without having to work I'd do it too, I think.

Once we were in Ketchikan, Alex asked me to skipper for him once more from Ketchikan down to Seattle the next month. I immediately agreed to it. I flew to Boston next to meet up with some of my family, and Alaina flew there from San Diego as her family was driving up from Florida for a 4th of July in New England as well. We flew back to San Diego later that week. Mat was right; Alaina hadn't been up to much, as I could see. No worries though, the bills were being paid, albeit out of her dad's pocket.

I had a few weeks before I had to go back to Ketchikan, so I skippered some charter boats out in San Diego Bay for a different and much more organized and professional charter boat company. I was having a pretty good time out there, even though the sailing wasn't quite what it was on the east coast, and I could see myself spending a year or two in California. Alaina had other ideas though and started nudging me towards the possibility of moving back east, a scant three months after we got out there. I could tell she was homesick and bored (hell, I would be too if I scrapbooked all day). The discussion was left open as I headed back to Alaska.

I met a different John, who would be with us on our passage through Canada. He was in his 50s and had his wife Sylvia in tow. They lived in San Francisco; he was an attorney, she was a professor at Berkeley. Together we all played lots of very intense Scrabble. The ten-or-so day passage went by quickly as we hopped from one port to another along the Canadian coast. We had a book with us that told the history of the explorer Vancouver and his explorations of this area, it was all fascinating: from the coves he anchored in, to the ruins and ghost towns that dotted the straits.

Once we were through the San Juan Islands and back in the States, we docked in Anacortes, Washington and made our way to Seattle. I was dropped at the airport and flew back to San Diego.

Alaina was still floundering and by this time really homesick. I had made up my mind as well; I was simply not a west coast kind of person. Although beautiful, the water was too cold for swimming throughout the year (call me spoiled but I can't stand wearing wetsuits). I had also discovered that the coastline is very stark, with only a few places to put in from Seattle all the way to San Diego and little to no gunkholing, which is one of the best parts of cruising in a small sailboat. The people were a little off-putting as well. Everyone thinks about California having a set of very laid back and chill citizens, and on the surface that's how it is. Dig a little deeper though, and you'll discover it's a medicated chill, one fabricated from the image itself and supported by a massive drug culture. Unemployment is rampant, and the only way they know how to deal with it is through escaping via substances. Take them away from those for a time, and they are high strung underneath it all, after the veneer of "chill" breaks away.

John and I making landfall in Sitka, Alaska

Contact with an iceberg (sans wetsuit), Glacier Bay, Alaska

XIII
Back to Florida

"The fishermen know that the sea is dangerous and the storm terrible, but they have never found these dangers sufficient reason for staying ashore." - Vincent van Gogh

It was settled then; we would move back east at the end of August. With the little bit of cash I had left, we decided to travel up the coast to San Francisco to see a friend and some of Alaina's family, then over to Lake Tahoe and Reno, down to the Grand Canyon and then a straight shot back east.

This, for better or worse, was when Alaina started to show her true colors. At every turn of inconvenience or compromise, her impatience and general disdain for anything that wasn't up to her level of satisfaction started to crack through the "free spirit" veneer she so skillfully sold me for the past eight months. I dismissed it to her being tired, both from the trip and of the double-coast move in general. We had a great time coming back across the country, my third transcontinental trip of the year.

Once we were back on the east coast, we stayed with her parents in Ft. Myers. Her dad had some odd jobs for me to do around the house while we got back on our feet. Alaina worked at her parent's furniture company. It was all a little emasculating, accepting money from her parents, and I wanted this phase of our relationship to be as short as possible. I was putting up and answering ads on craigslist and other sites requesting captain services, but to mostly no avail. The most promising thing I found was up in Bradenton, where my mother lived, a two hour drive from Ft. Myers. Funny thing was, Alaina wouldn't leave her parents. Every day it was something new. Her sister had a 7 year old daughter and between her, Alaina's older sister and her two kids and husband (who still lived out of her parent's pocket), her parents needing something, etc., etc., there was no way to get out of the general logistics nightmare that was her family. I had to frequently commute from her place up to this fledgling charter business I was trying to start with a few other guys with a couple of boats near Anna Maria Island. It was tough, and I can't say she made it any easier.

A year to the day after declaring *Winchelsea* dead (to me and my situation), I was living aboard again. She was Alaina's father's Gulfstar 41; a heavy, solid cruising boat with a well-appointed, yet simple, interior. He kept her in Ft. Myers for the past few years while restoring and improving some of the more aged parts of the vessel. Allowing me to liveaboard in Sarasota was mutually beneficial; he has wanted to keep her in Sarasota for a season ever since he got the yacht, and it is pretty pricey to dock a boat at Marina Jacks. This way, he would have someone with experience to watch over her and complete a few projects, and I'd have a place to live in Sarasota, thank God, on a boat again.

We dropped the hook in Sarasota Bay after coming up outside of Sanibel and Captiva islands and into

Venice inlet. It was a two day trip with a stop near Cabbage Key; a picturesque island in Pine Island Sound just north of Ft. Myers. This is exactly what I came back east for: gunkholing, which is the simple pleasure of meandering from cove to cove, only sailing a few miles each day. I'd had the desire to gunk in the area I grew up ever since buying *Winchelsea* was a passing thought back in Boston.

Wow, Boston. It seemed like a long time ago then, but it was less than two years in the past. Thinking back to the desk job, I marveled at how quickly the days, weeks and months congealed into an amorphous blur. Did I go sailing yesterday, or last week? It's winter again *already??* Recalling all I did in the past 22 months, however, was a breeze. I could distinctly remember each month, almost every week and a lot of specific days. I remembered all the steps that it took to get where I was then, instead of an endless cycle of sleepwalking for five days punctuated by two to call "my own," repeat until death. And honestly, it felt a lot more like two years should.

In the end, this arrangement worked for a bit, but Alaina's reluctance to find a job given the inconvenience of rowing to shore and walking 200 yards to a shower (but instead driving 15 minutes to her sister's place) made a short time of that.

Since I was back in the town I grew up in, and I thought we'd be staying there for a while, I thought I'd get involved in some local issues that affected the cruising community. The concept of trying to control the waters off of certain areas of desirable coastline is nothing new, and Sarasota is no exception. Before 2009, the local municipalities could make ordinances to limit the amount of time a boat could spend anchored in the limits of their fine city. That all changed when the Florida legislature deemed those ordinances unconstitutional. They also changed the definition of a live-aboard to one who uses a vessel strictly for a home, and a cruiser as someone who may reside on their boat, but also navigates. The difference being that a cruisers boat can move under its own power whereas liveaboard's can't. Under the current laws, it is legal to cruise and illegal to liveaboard. This is fine by me; it keeps boats that shouldn't be inhabited, out of the water. There is also a law on the books that allows cities to create and maintain mooring fields. Again, no problems there.

What I do have an issue with, and what there were multiple meetings about at the Sarasota City Hall, is the creation of ordinances that regulate a cruiser's right to anchor *outside* of those designated mooring areas. We, as sailors, have a right to navigate on any of the waters in the United States. And, anchoring is part of that navigation. The general consensus of the cruisers attending city commission meetings was that there does not need to be any more regulation than is already on the books. The city commissioners were talking of making a time limit and/or "buffer zones" around the mooring field (one proposal by a local marine corporation, Marina Jack, calls for 5 miles and a time limit of 1 hour). In addition, they are charging $270 to $345 per month for a mooring ball! I was assured by the project manager for the construction of the mooring field that there is "no profit associated with the mooring field. It was grant money from the EPA and as part of the grant's stipulations; any excess revenue has to go directly back into the mooring field program." So Marina Jack is doing this without keeping any profits for themselves? How wonderful! *Yeah, I don't think so either.* What I spoke on record about and proposed, with a lot of other people saying just about the same thing, was that what Sarasota needs is a harbormaster. I outlined a system similar to Newport, where there are designated mooring fields and a designated anchorage as well. The system is regulated and enforced by a harbormaster who takes down your information, including a cell phone contact number, when you enter the anchorage and calls you if there is an issue. What Sarasota was trying to do is create a solution to a problem that didn't exist. I've been in anchorages and seen many derelict boats, sailboats without masts and blue tarps over cabin tops to keep the rain out, and Sarasota had none of these.

It was also at one of these meetings I learned what had happened to *Terrapin Flyer* and, much more importantly, Alex.

I got a phone call from Alex in mid-October. His boat, the *Terrapin Flyer,* which I had sailed with him from Hawaii to Alaska and down to Seattle, was in southern Washington and he needed to get it down to San Francisco by the end of the month. Unfortunately, he wouldn't be able to join me on the trip and responsibility would be all on me this time. I told him I would be more than happy to do the delivery for him. Looking at the pilot charts though, and reading about the typical conditions off of the Oregon coast at this time of year, it would be no walk in the park. Gales are frequent as are seas over 12 feet. No, this wouldn't be easy, but it would be an awesome challenge. Fate was not with me to do this delivery though; I got a call from a guy I had been trying to start a charter business with in Bradenton and he had already made the print material for a grand opening on October 22nd.

John, the southern chef from the Hawaii - Alaska trip was going to crew on the delivery, and I'll admit I was pretty jealous. He called me after the delivery was completed, and I was excited and relieved to see his name pop up on my phone. He started to tell me about the trip, but there was a tone in his voice that told me something wasn't right with how things turned out. The boat was fine; he assured me, as was all crew that made the trip. For two days, their second and third day out from Washington, *Terrapin Flyer* was battered with gusts of wind to 50 knots and choppy, angry seas. They took in all of the genoa outside of a small postage stamp flying from the headstay and as much of the main as they could to maintain some balance of the yacht. Back in California, it was equally as turbulent. The reason Alex could not make the trip was a due to a heart attack he had a month earlier. He had a coronary angioplasty performed, but part of his heart was damaged. And, as *Terrapin Flyer* was pounded in the Pacific, Alex passed away at his home in California. As John entered cell phone range coming into San Francisco, he learned of the terrible news. I can't think of a worse way to come into a port after such an exciting trip. Alex was only 40.

A couple of weeks passed, and I unexpectedly got a message on Facebook from John Sullivan saying that *Terrapin* had been broken into sitting in her berth in Oakland and that the family wanted her moved to San Diego, ASAP. He said that Tom would be bringing her south with me, the captain who took the boat down from Washington when I couldn't make it. I got in touch with Tom just before Thanksgiving and flew out the following Tuesday. John Sullivan picked me up from the airport in Oakland Tuesday evening.

We were all up at six in the morning the next day and motoring out of Golden Gate by about eight. The wind was flat calm as we puttered along out of the bay and into the Pacific. There was a hefty five foot swell from the north though, and by noon we had turned her south and a steady 15 knot breeze had filled in behind us. The rest of the day was uneventful outside of the naps, conversation and snacking that most cruises start out with. The shifts were divided into a 4 hour on, 8 hour off schedule and I had the 4 to 8 (both AM and PM) shifts. When I turned in at 8 in the evening, the stars were out, the temperature had dropped and the wind had picked up to a gusty 25 knots. I woke up at about 3:50 in the morning, and the boat was moving around a lot more than it had when I left the cockpit the night before. I hollered up to Tom about what the conditions were like, and he replied with a simple "cold and pretty windy." I looked at the anemometer, and it was a steady 30 to 35 knots with gusts to just over 40. Windy it was. It didn't feel uncomfortable or unsafe though, there was a double reef in the main and the jib was rolled up; the head sail was unnecessary as we were headed almost directly downwind. Tom advised that I watch the main to be sure it didn't backwind. It wouldn't gybe over because we had the preventer in tight.

Motoring under the Golden Gate Bridge with fog

The next few hours passed slowly as I waited for the sun to rise. The wind was still increasing and at about 6:30, when the sky was a light, pre-dawn grey, taking a look around I could finally see the sea state. It was jaw-dropping. Twenty to 22 foot faces were following us, towering over our stern like being chased by a wall of water the size of a two-story building. After watching this for 30 minutes, with the light still increasing, I observed something I had only heard about previously. Around 7 AM, I was looking off the starboard stern quarter when I saw a gust coming that literally chopped the tops off of these 22 foot monsters, one after another, like the side of a giant, ethereal hand was at work. I quickly headed about 10 degrees to windward (thank God the autopilot was still working during all this) as the gust approached. The wind speed indicator read 46 knots apparent, and we were doing about 10 knots downwind at the time. A 56 knot gust. The boat heeled over, rails deep in green water, and the rigging hummed and quivered with strain, but she recovered quickly.

It was time to gybe. We had been heading offshore, in more of a south-southwest direction, and it was time to head back in towards Point Conception and the Santa Barbara Channel. I woke up Tom and John. Tom took the wheel to hand steer while I released the preventer, hauled the main in and freed the traveler. Tom steered slowly to port, and the boom came over as we gybed in a trough between the waves. Next came the task of resetting the preventer and, since I was a solid 35 years younger than either of my crewmates, I'll give you a guess as to who got to leave the cockpit to do so. Hunched over on the leeward rail, feeding a line through a snatch block to bring back to the cockpit, the boat heeled over from a gust drenching me from the waist down in water that was moving at nearly 10 knots. I saw it coming though, and braced myself securely. I made my way back to the cockpit and rolled in. It was now 8 AM and my shift was over. I went below, removed my soaked foulies and crawled into my bunk.

By my next shift, the seas were down considerably, as well as the winds. Reflecting on the previous shift, it was surreal and intense, but never did I feel the boat was out of control or fearful. Tom is an excellent and experienced captain, and I was very glad he was aboard for an experience like that. By the next morning, the wind had dropped completely. We were past the Channel Islands, motoring towards Catalina with San Diego a short 75 miles beyond that.

I was on watch the morning after as we rounded Point Loma and headed into San Diego Bay. We motored into her slip and started cleaning. Everything was caked with salt, and the cabin was still a mess from the journey. The next day Alex's widow and his parents came to see the boat. There was a lot of emotion, and I did my best to not act too awkward in an already awkward situation. I just told them stories about the trips from this past summer with Alex and how great it was to have the opportunity to sail on such a fantastic yacht with such wonderful company. They left, and Tom went to dinner late in the afternoon.

As so it ends. While it would be nice to think I'd be sailing on her again someday, I know that probably won't happen. That boat and, more importantly, its owner changed my life. They offered me the opportunity of a first ocean passage, meeting the great people he surrounded himself with and a myriad of memories.

Leaving Terrapin Flyer *in San Diego*

Eventually, Alaina and I settled on a place in downtown Sarasota after the New Year, 2012. I had hung up my sailing spurs though, and was focusing on tutoring and applying to teaching and engineering jobs. I was planning on putting the cruising lifestyle on hold for a bit; we needed money because as far as I know that's the only way to get even a half decent boat. I also did something I hadn't really put a lot of forethought into, I proposed. But hey, isn't that something you're not *supposed* to put a lot of forethought into?

So there we were, a happily, newly engaged couple living in a small, cute apartment in the downtown area of Sarasota. Over the next couple of months, I banged my head against the wall and applied to well over 40 legitimate jobs. Engineering, teaching, manufac-turing, office work, you name it. There was no job too low for me. I just wanted something to do, some stable income and a chance at saving for a boat.

By this time, my idea of a perfect boat had fi-nally materialized. I wanted a smaller boat; *Winchelsea* was too big. Something closer to 30' would be much more manageable. I also liked the idea of a divided sail plan, as in a ketch rig, and, of course, a full keel. A tran-som hung rudder would also be nice, for the sake of simplicity. These specifications did not come without influence. I had read all of Bernard Moistessier's works, as well as most by Tristan Jones, the Pardeys, John Vigor and Hal Roth to name a few. Admittedly, I didn't have a lot of experience sailing a boat that I had dreamed of, but I had a good amount of faith in those opinions I was reading about.

While I kept banging away at finding gainful em-ployment, and tutoring part time to pay the bills, Alaina had got a job at a gym. A gym with an owner of a mixed reputation. Since we were now engaged, I was trying to wean Alaina off of her parent's cash teat. She still couldn't pay her half of the bills on her own, which I told her was marginally acceptable since we were en-gaged but would cease to be once the knot was tied. I was reassuring in explaining that we had as much time as we needed; we didn't have to get married any time before we were good and ready, but she was concerned that "2012" sounded so much better than "2013" on the invitations.

Sailing-wise, for those first few months of 2012, I

was restoring a 505 and building a 19 foot Norseboat with a friend Dillon, who I actually met in Newport. He had a great couple of spaces to work in and was a bonafide naval architect. I also got into racing a little bit with a couple of friends, Sean and Travis, on his parents 41' Bristol. We did a couple of buoy races and a coastal race down to Venice and back.

Around mid-April, I walked the docks in Sarasota and stumbled upon a newly resurrected business. There was a fishing charter business that I hadn't seen there in years just starting up again. I sure as Hell didn't know much about fishing, but I decided to give it a go. After meeting with the owner, he agreed to hire me on temporarily, without pay, while I "learned the ropes." He was very vague with what that meant, which translated to "I'm going to work you as long as I can without pay." Not something I was accustomed to.

That first day was something I wasn't accustomed to either. I was on a giant fishing boat for hire, with one captain, one crew, the intern (me), and a cocktail waitress who didn't know her ass from her elbow. Once we were at the "spot" every dip shit tourist on the boat (and I had dealt with many, many tourists before, these were by far the worst) dropped their lines and one after another, started bringing up fish I wouldn't be proud to show my dog. But, doing my duty, I grabbed a rag and started picking them up and stringing them on numbers I told them to remember. About half way through the day the "captain" came down and told me to ditch the rag. I told him these damn fish were slippery, and I was tired of chasing them around the deck.

He then belittled me in front of the passengers (as far as I know, the LAST thing you do on a charter vessel) and began to pick a fight with the "mate."

I went home that night with a pit in my stomach. I knew I couldn't do that again tomorrow, especially without pay and not even knowing *when* I would get paid. I had to pick Matt up at the airport that night, the same Matt who I went to Los Angeles with before my *Terrapin Flyer* adventure. He always had a knack for being there during major transitions in my life. Long story short, we got drunk, and I didn't go back to that shitty fishing boat the next day. Alaina was more than pissed. Matt left the day after, and her wrath was harsh. Her boss, at the gym she worked at, said it sounded like a great job and she said he was disappointed that I didn't work it out. She was starting to listen to him a lot, and spend some serious time outside of work with him, which I didn't exactly find comforting.

As luck would have it, I got a call after Matt left to sail out of St. Maarten the day after next. The boat was going to Newport via Bermuda. It was called *Amerigo,* and it would change my life, once again. I packed my duffel and Alaina and I had dinner at a local burger shack before I went to my mother's place, who offered to drive me to Tampa the next day (bless her soul, once she realized how happy sailing and my life-style change had made me was she was extremely supportive). Before I left, I leveled with Alaina. I could feel the tension between us. She didn't want to leave the comfort of her family's pocketbook, and I couldn't see myself living the same way. The frustration started to come out in different ways, such as (and I'm not exaggerating) leaving the toilet seat up. I was also writing some of this book at the time, sometimes well into the night, which she wasn't pleased with. I couldn't exactly figure out why.

Flying over the Bahamas to St. Maarten I pictured myself down there, in *Winchelsea* or whatever boat I might have in the future. It was all so simple, the idea I had when I left Boston. Just to sail down here, to Florida, and through the Bahamas. It had taken me a long time at this point, and I still wasn't sure how I'd get back there.

I arrived in St. Maarten and took a cab from the airport to the marina in Simpson Bay. This, of course, was not without issue. The cab driver dropped me off at the wrong place and refused to bring me to the marina. I found a bar and asked the guy working there to call me another cab. The boat *Amerigo* is a 56' Swan, an extremely high end yacht, good for racing, cruising, entertaining and, and I was to find out, crewing aboard. Grant, the captain who was from Scotland and only a few weeks older than myself, and I got the boat ready to depart in a few days and welcomed the owner and the other delivery crew member aboard on the evening before departure. I also talked with Alaina that evening, and nothing seemed out of the ordinary. This was a Tuesday.

We left on a Wednesday morning with clear skies. They remained clear with the trades pushing us north at a quite respectable 9 knots for most of the trip. It felt great to be back on the water again, which I hadn't been since December. I passed the time reading a lot. There were four of us, so the watch schedule was moderate and relaxed. Our second night at sea I had a very vivid dream. I dreamed that Alaina was at a party and being sexually assaulted by her boss at the gym. It shook me so much, that I prompted Grant if I could call my fiancé from the satellite phone the next morning. When I got through, there was something different in her voice, uneasiness. She assured me she was alright though, and given the cost per minute of the call, I had to cut it off there.

The only weather we ran into was the night before we made landfall. The wind piped up to about 30 knots on our stern, which made for some great sailing. I don't know if anyone reading this will ever have the opportunity to sail a Swan downwind, with about 20 apparent knots, surfing 8 to 10 foot seas into Bermuda as the sun rises, but if you do, I suggest you take it. We took the sails down, motored into St George's and tied up at the customs dock.

After checking in, we went to the yachting center to find some internet and make contact with loved ones. I got onto G-chat and immediately found Alaina was online. I asked her if anything was wrong. She replied there was and that the engagement was over. Just like that. I had to see the owner and another crew member off to the airport and in a weird, shell-shocked daze stumbled around to find a phone to call the States. Once I called her, she affirmed it was true. She explained she had an enjoyable time without me around the past few days and decided it was over. I didn't argue.

I only asked how we were splitting up the apartment and all that stuff. She said she'd take over the rent, excellent.

After lunch and a very, very much needed Dark and Stormy I asked Grant what the plan was for *Amerigo*. He said he'd continue to Newport once the weather was favorable, which didn't look like was going to happen for another week. I told him my situation, and he offered a round trip from Bermuda back to Florida to get my stuff moved out, and a spot on *Amerigo* to continue to Newport. Well, I certainly didn't have any reason to go back to Florida now, and I knew a bunch of people in Newport, so it was settled right there.

After a raucous night celebrating my newly found singledom with the crew of the *Picton Castle* and her busty boatswain, I departed for Florida. I got back to Sarasota at 2 am the next night and found the apartment empty. It was a disaster, with the lights left on, dishes piled in the sink, heaps of clothes everywhere. No ex-fiancée to be found. I loaded everything I owned into the back of my Geo Metro, including the ring in my pocket that I had found in the dresser drawer, and headed back to Mom's house. On the way to the airport the next morning I got a call from Alaina, in distress, asking if I had a friend move my stuff out. I confirmed that no, it was me, and that I was on my way back to Bermuda.

XIV
A Change in Heading

"Alice came to a fork in the road. 'Which road do I take?'
she asked.
'Where do you want to go?' responded the Cheshire Cat.
'I don't know,' Alice answered.
'Then,' said the Cat, 'it doesn't matter."
- Lewis Carroll, *Alice in Wonderland*

I found Grant at the exact same place I had left him,
Dark and Stormy in hand at the White Horse Tavern.
We had another few days to wait for the weather, and
his list of potential crew was growing small. I called my
friend Geoff, and he arrived Monday at 2:30 in the afternoon. We were underway at 4. I knew Geoff from
Newport a couple of seasons ago; he worked on the
schooner *Madeline* next to *Aquidneck*. The first after-
noon/night we had a fair 15 knot breeze out of the
northeast, so we were close reaching on a good course
to Newport. The wind fell the next day, and we motored for most of it, nothing special. Tuesday night,
however, the wind backed to the southwest and really
started to fill in. By the time my 6 am watch came
around it was sustained at nearly 30 knots and the seas
had risen considerably. We had two reefs in the main
and only the small staysail up and were still flying along
at over 9 knots with the wind on our beam.

Over the next 36 hours, it kept its strength (gusting to 36 according to the anemometer) but veered

around to the north. We followed it as best we could, but were forced to tack, and did so another two times. We were in the Gulf Stream at this point and fighting a three knot current. The seas were very confused, with the changing wind directions and a strong current; it was like a washing machine, with 12 foot waves. *Amerigo* slammed into one wave while another gently pushed its stern, only to have another smack its beam seconds later to send water all the way back to the cockpit. A Cory's shearwater, similar to an albatross, followed us Thursday afternoon as the winds and seas finally started to ease. We motored the remainder of the way into Newport and arrived on the morning of May 5th.

After clearing customs I met up with Green, former captain of *Aquidneck* and current Captain of *Madeline*. He introduced me to the manager of *Madeline* and within hours of hitting the dock in Newport, I had a job. This was a stark contrast to banging my head against a wall for months trying to find gainful employment in Sarasota. This was a great gig, one I had done before and knew well. However, some bizarre new policy was implemented that only allowed 30 hours, spread over 6 days, of work per week… something about us not getting "burned out." I had worked 12 hour days in past seasons and didn't know why this was any different. I was keeping my options open for something else to come along; by sheer luck, the captain of *Amerigo* put me in touch with a friend of his, who then forwarded my info and experience on to her captain on *Whitehawk,* who then got me in touch with the captain of

Sumurun, who was looking for deckhands, as well as a mate. I met him the very next morning, and he immediately asked if I would come for a sail on Friday and Saturday. I accepted graciously.

Sumurun is an amazing yacht. I remembered it from two summers previous since we would point it out to passengers on *Aquidneck* as one of the most well-kept and breathtaking yachts in the harbor. It is 94 feet in length overall and nearly 100 years old. More of a floating, functioning museum of the days of yachting past kept in perfect condition; at a glance you would probably guess it was built less than a decade ago. It sails like a demon on rails to boot. And, after the weekend sailing and spending time with the wonderful crew, I took a full-time position that was offered to me. It was a fantastic deal, with a salary, room and board as well as health benefits. In exchange, the days are long when the owner is aboard, and my free time was very limited and unpredictable.

After a month living in a space with six people no larger than *Winchelsea*, I had had enough. "Sailing" as the owner called it, meant bobbing around if there was wind or not in the sweltering heat while we served lunch to him, his family and guests. Not exactly what I had signed up for. The captain was also having an affair with the cook, and when he went home to his wife and kids, the cook was left in charge. Shit hit the fan. Her style of management was through demeaning insults and sarcasm. I took her aside one afternoon and asked her to knock it off, I didn't find it professional, and it was hard enough living in those conditions, let alone walking on eggshells the whole time. The captain came back a few days later and fired me. Good riddance.

So there I was, midsummer in Newport with no job and all seasonal sailing positions filled. After the delivery and my month on *Sumurun* I had about $7,000 saved up, plus a ring valued at $1,000. As per my usual hobby, I was perusing craigslist one night and came across something interesting. It was an ad for an early model Allied Seawind in Rhode Island. I took a look at the specs again and confirmed that it was indeed something that matched my requirements for a boat perfectly.

The asking price was $10,000 and the ad said it needed some work. With that phrase of "needing work" I knew there was some room for negotiation. Matt, who again always seems to come around whenever I am nearing a transition in my life, drove me to Watch Hill two days later to take a look at it. It was on a mooring, and the manager of the marina told me it had arrived here by tow in late winter and, after finally figuring out who the owner was, convinced him to sell it. Matt and I went out to look at it and from just approaching the boat the fact that it "needed work" was not only true, but quite an understatement.

There were no sails bent on, and the mizzen boom was in the cabin. The cabin looked (and smelled) like a troop of vagrant hobos had been living in her (which was actually the case, I came to find out). The holding tank was disconnected and sitting on deck. The lifelines were rusty and fraying. There was no fresh water system. The bowsprit was rotten and half missing.

There were no cushions in the entire boat. The engine was inoperable for a number of reasons that started with a broken key in the ignition. The whole boat needed to be rewired. The deck was stained from the rusted ground tackle that had been sitting for some time. There was no dinghy or outboard. Overall, she needed serious cosmetic work including paint on the bottom, topsides, deck and interior.

However, and most importantly, the hull and decks were solid and the engine was a small European diesel I could still get parts for. The sails were there, but they were tired. Matt thought I was nuts, but I knew I had found my boat. On the trip back to Newport, I devised my strategy. I would call the owner late the following day and tell him that I may be interested in the boat; I just had to work out the numbers, which was actually very true. I had a pretty good idea of the cost to get this thing up to snuff. A few days later I called him up and offered $2,500, plus a gold and sapphire ring worth at least $500. He accepted immediately.

The next week I wired him the money and flew down to Florida. I threw everything I owned into the back of the aging Metro and said a prayer that I'd make it to Rhode Island in this thing. Everything also included a dinghy and outboard, kind of amazing if you think about it. That drive was a spiritual journey. No A/C, no radio, just me and the midsummer Florida heat starting a true voyage...with a flat tire. It was impossible to find a 12" spare in Sarasota, and I had to drive to Orlando to find one. After a night there with my brother, playing poker with his friends, I was on the road at 4am.

Things were going swimmingly until a fuel filter issue almost stopped me dead on I-75 in North Carolina. That damned state. I arrived in Washington DC at two the following morning at a friend's house. On the road again at eight, onto New Jersey to meet up with, you guessed it, Matt Hartke. I attended his sister's graduation party that evening and the next day I completed the trip back to Rhode Island and spent my first night on my new boat.

The next morning the boat and I were towed to a dock. I was told I had just about a week to get it in shape enough to sail to where ever I needed to, but that I couldn't stay there. My first move was removing no less than two dozen trash bags full of crap off the boat and straight into the dumpster, thankful to now have the knowledge of what was good to keep and what wasn't.

Next, I needed to get some running rigging since there was none on board. Asking around for a marine consignment store, I picked up two sets of block and tackle for the main and mizzen sheets. West Marine was next for the halyards and jib sheets. I got back to the boat and had the sails bent on, and lines run by the afternoon and uncovered some sail covers that were still in decent shape. She was starting to look like a boat! I got the engine running with a spare can of diesel the marina had around (the one the boat was full of 10 gallons of bad fuel I had to pump out manually) and realized that 1) the transmission was stuck in forward and 2) there was no water coming out the back. I removed the water pump and found the impeller was completely shot, and that the bearings, seals, and a new impeller were not available domestically. It was sent off to be rebuilt. The transmission was a big issue that would have to wait. The holding tank sitting on deck was tossed out, as was the extremely permeable hose that led from it to the toilet. This made things down below much more pleasant. A four inch foam mattress topper and some new bedding for the V-berth rounded out the basic essentials.

The maiden voyage of *Soveraine* started with a quote, as we all piled into the Metro in Newport, bound for Watch Hill, "your souls had better belong to Jesus boys, because your asses are mine." Not sure where I had heard that before, but I figured it was appropriate given that I apparently have a reputation for wild adventures on the high (and in this case not so high) seas.

Dan and Seabass (Captain Seabass) had agreed to share in this adventure since they both had off the following day. It took about an hour to get down there, and since it was where Seabass grew up, we stopped into a place where he knew the owner and had some $1 tacos and margaritas when we got there. I attempted to put on a collared shirt, but was promptly told that this was not that kind of place. Nine tacos and eight margaritas later we piled back into the Metro for a couple of miles to the boatyard.

5:15 am came early the next day. Sunrise was at 5:30 and we were puttering along at 5:45. I had the dinghy hip-tied to the boat amidships and the little three and a half horsepower "outboard that could" pushed the six ton vessel along at about two knots, with only one-third of the throttle. Within an hour, we were out of the channel and another hour after that we passed Watch Hill lighthouse that marks the reef. Trouble was there was still no wind. The dinghy stayed hip-tied, and we kept on towards Point Judith. At one point, Dan decided to go swimming.

Dan and I sailing to Newport from Watch Hill, RI

We finished off the two beers left on board from the previous night with lunch and quickly realized that we had under provisioned for this trip. Discussing options such as pulling up to a beach, dropping the hook and taking the dinghy ashore, or pulling into Point Judith, it was decided the most logical plan would be to hail a passing boat for some emergency supplies. A 26' cat boat passed us not too long after, and I was elected to untie the dinghy and motor over. The captain graciously gave us two beers each and we chatted about sail configurations awhile before I made my way back to my thirsty crew.

Seabass and I on the maiden voyage to Newport

Finally, at about 2:30 that afternoon, the sea breeze kicked in and gave us a nice southwesterly to allow us to raise all sail, reach past Point Judith and run into Narragansett Bay. We dropped the hook at about eight PM after one attempt failed due to a disgruntled cruiser claiming we had just dropped ours on top of his.

Not wanting to argue (or have someone like that as my neighbor) we pulled it up and reset further in.

I had quite the rush of emotion sailing my own small boat into Narragansett Bay and Newport again, after doing so with *Winchelsea* over two years prior. Despite all that has happened in 2012, both up north and in Florida, I felt calm, at peace and at home there; swinging on the end of a hook and chain, listening to the fog horns and being gently rocked to sleep in the small piece of this crazy world I can call my own. I don't think I can say for certain whether I saved this boat or if this boat saved me.

I went back and forth for a long time trying to decide on an appropriate name for my new old vessel. I first toyed with family names, such as Andrew for my departed cousin and Beatrice for my Grammy. Neither of these would work though, just too close to home. I then thought of past loves and deemed none of them appropriate either.

Bernard Moitessier, my favorite sailor and author of all time ever, had named his boat *Joshua* after his own favorite sailor Joshua Slocum. Could I name my boat Bernard? I mean, if such a great sailor could give his boat a masculine name, then I surely could as well. I thought I had made up my mind, but I just couldn't shake the thought of my boat not being feminine. I decided I would sail her first to truly let her make my mind up, and after the trip from Watch Hill to Newport, I knew it had to be a lady.

But what could the name be? I thought I'd try and incorporate what my goals with this boat are: self-sufficiency. I found a thesaurus and the word sovereignty came up. I liked that word, for a nation it means controlling resources without the coercion of other nations. On an individual level, it means having the liberty to decide one's own thoughts and actions. Perfect. Google translator came up with Summus. Hmmm...way too close to *Sumurun* and still too masculine. So I looked to the etymology of sovereignty and found it comes from an old, old French word (like from 1100 AD) soverain. The female form of which is soveraine.

So, the name is French as a tip of the hat to Mr. Moitessier. It is feminine and almost has a name-like quality to it while still keeping the meaning of autonomy.

Soveraine, hailing from Newport.

After I managed to get *Soveraine* to Newport, I needed to find a job for the remainder of the season. My funds from the original $7,000 had almost completely evaporated by this point. I applied to be a launch driver for the New York Yacht Club at Harbor Court (which you have to say with your teeth clenched to get the full effect), but the pay was lousy, I wouldn't be sailing and not allowed to accept tips! A good friend Micah, who worked on another 12 meter, told me a spot had just opened up on *Weatherly*, whose claim to fame is winning the 1962 America's Cup. I sent in my resume and within two days was sailing with them and offered a full time position for the remainder of the season. Somehow, I always managed to land on my feet. Either through tenacity, a positive attitude, sheer dumb luck, or most likely a combination of the three, it works out.

Weatherly was designed by Phillip Rhodes, who also designed the Rhodes 19, the boat I learned to sail on in Boston Harbor. It was the only 12 meter to win the America's Cup designed by him (the rest by Sparkman and Stephens also based in Newport). She's gorgeous under sail; sailing on the schooners I'd always admired the 12 meters, their lines and grace in the water. They develop a large, pronounced trough that extends the length of the water line on the windward side when they reach hull speed, which is something that has to be seen to appreciate fully.

I was crew on *Weatherly* for the remainder of the 2012 season. We went to Martha's Vineyard and Nantucket for a handful of regattas, and I got my first taste of big boat racing. Much different is about all I can say. Everything is larger, heavier and more physical aboard larger yachts. The #1 genoa takes 3 people to haul up on deck, which is a tall order when it's also hanked on and has to be switched out on a downwind leg when you are also trying to gybe the spinnaker at the same time. This is also where I got my nickname "Scotty Do". Tom, my fellow crewmate who showed me all about 12 meter sailing, gave it to me during the regattas, saying "Scotty do this and Scotty do that." Fitting, I suppose.

Weatherly, Columbia and American Eagle *at Edgartown, Martha's Vineyard, August 2013*
Photo: Kelsy Patnaude

Sailing on Weatherly *is a blast, I'm forward in white*

I made some great friends during the last half of that 2012 season. All of the captains and crews on the eight or so active 12 meter boats know each other very well and form a pretty tight knit group. Some may say they have arrogant chips on their shoulders, but in a few cases its justified. George and Herb, captains and owners of *Weatherly* and *American Eagle* respectively, are masters. They have both been sailing 12 meters together in the northeast for the better part of three decades and it really shows. Their incredible command over their yachts and racing them to the brink (with a crew who is not always top notch, myself included) is nothing short of awe inspiring. The amount I learned from these guys, especially George, could be a book in itself.

***

I am a firm believer in a higher power at work in the universe. Like of a flow of energy, akin to a current in a channel or a trade wind, you can either go with it or try to beat against it. And when you're going with that flow, the universe responds in kind.

Back in July, before I bought *Soveraine,* I found an online picture album of Scott and Kitty, a couple who made their way around the world in an Allied Seawind called *Bebinka* in the early 1970s. It took them three years, and they took a lot of pictures. Recently they posted them all to the web complete with captions, which I read in their entirety before purchasing *Soveraine.*

In August, after I returned from my cousin's wedding in New York, I got up early the next morning determined to get the engine running. I went out and bought a new fuel tank with the materials to install it and got back to the boat at about 11 am. I was below when I heard a knock on the hull and someone say, "Allied Seawind! You in there?"

I popped up to see an older man in his dinghy beside my boat. He told me that he and his wife had circumnavigated in another Allied Seawind back in 1971. "In *Bebinka*?" I replied, "Are you Scott and is your wife Kitty??!?"

He nearly fell out of his dinghy, clean into Newport harbor. We were both speechless for a moment, just kind of staring at each other. I was imagining this guy, now in his early 70s, how he looked in those pictures at 30, embarking on a voyage around the world in a nearly identical craft. He gazed right back, seeing himself in me some 40 years ago.

"You have to come to our boat for coffee!" He exclaimed, and pointed to a Valiant 40 anchored just off my bow.

"I'll be over in a heartbeat!"

I could hear from across the water as he got to *Tamure*, "Kitty! He's coming over for coffee! He's heard of us and seen our whole voyage on the internet!"

It was surreal seeing these two together and being in their cabin after reading those picture captions about their voyage from so long ago. It was as if there were no middle aged years; I "saw" Scott and Kitty when they were 30 and 25, newly married and glowing with youth. They were still glowing, for sure, from a lifetime of sailing and adventure.

We spent the entire afternoon talking about absolutely everything. They asked me what plans I had for my boat, and I told them about my goals of self-reliance and to start by voyaging in the Bahamas starting next fall. I picked their brains about rigging for my boat (among other things including the galley, electrical system, their engine, etc.), including a twin jib configuration they used frequently, running with the trades on both of their circumnavigations. They still use the exact same wind vane on their Valiant 40.

Scott came to see my boat as well, giving me a lot of pointers to fixing her up and doing it right. He got very quiet as he came below into my then quite barren cabin. He looked around silently, and then to me, and I could see that gaze of reflection, as if looking into a 40 year old mirror.

They left the next day, bound for home in Connecticut, and then on to the Bahamas in early October. It was relieving to see them, now in their late 60s and early 70s, still doing what they love and to be still so in love with each other. I told them how privileged I felt to have met my own personal Larry and Lin Pardey, and in such a fateful way. They said they felt similar, and they were relieved to see that young people like myself are still doing what they set out to do, at almost the exact same age and on the same vessel even, some 40 years ago.

It was about this same time I had yet another incident with my dinghy, this time involving law enforcement. I left the local pub Benjamin's at about midnight one night in midsummer. It was a short walk to the Ann

Street dinghy dock a quarter of a mile away and, unbeknownst to me at the time, I was being followed. When I arrived at my humble floating chariot, I pumped out the water, pumped up the port side tube that never stays inflated, hopped in and pushed away from the dock to start the engine. Within seconds, three bright beams of light illuminated me, in front of a stern voice instructing me to return to the dock. I didn't panic though that's exactly what they want you to do. They're looking for a reason to throw the book at you; the trick is to never give them the opportunity. I obliged and was informed I was too intoxicated to operate the vessel.

Now, I'll admit I had a few at old Benji's, but I really didn't think I was impaired in any way. I asked if I could simply row to my boat and got a reply to the effect of they didn't trust me that I wouldn't start the engine once I turned the corner. They were probably right. Anywho, they dragged the dinghy up onto the dock, completely deflated her and threw me in the back of the squad car. I wasn't handcuffed or read my rights, was I being arrested?

"You're not under arrest, we're taking you home."

"Well, my boat is my home, so I don't know where you plan to take me."

"We'll take you to a hotel."

"OK, fine by me!"

I had never been in the back of a police vehicle; it was like a taxi with bars and really hard seats. This was about when I updated my Facebook status, saying I had been arrested for a flare of drama. When we arrived

145

at the hotel, I was escorted in with one of the officers and the lady at the desk said it would be $120. I looked to the officer.

Me: "Go ahead sir."

Cop: "We're not buying you a hotel room. Pay the woman."

Me: "Well, I only have $60 in my checking account."

Desk lady: "That's the best price I can do."

Cop (looking to me): "Are you joking?"

Me: "I wish I was. I'm sorry; I'm not trying to mess with you, I just don't have any money."

Cop (with a very heavy eye roll): "Get back in the damn car."

They drove me around for another hour, even went on another call, before dropping me off in a Wal-Mart parking lot at 1 AM. An eventful evening that did not end as poorly as I had thought when I first saw those flashlights. A friend was just getting out of work at a restaurant and came and picked me up.

The real kicker was when I got back to the dinghy in the morning. The tide had come up during the night and crushed my engine between the floating dock they put her on and the gangway ramp. The pull cord wouldn't pull, so I rowed back to *Soveraine* and spent the next hour disassembling the housing and bending it back into shape.

XV
Another New England Winter

"If anything's gonna happen, it's gonna happen out there." - Captain Ron, *Captain Ron*

In late August, I made the decision that I would be spending the winter in Newport. *Soveraine* and I were just not ready to make the trip yet. I'd only had her out sailing twice, and I needed to get more time with her before I could spend my limited resources on a 1,500 mile trip to Florida. Not to mention, when I got to Florida I'd be broke and back in a state with limited employment opportunities. I got the engine started again after a new fuel tank, filters, lines, a rebuilt water pump, cleaning the heat exchanger, changing the oil, etc., but the gearbox was still stuck in forward. According to people in the know I'd talked to the discs were warped, and it needed to be rebuilt. The bowsprit and bobstay still needed to be replaced as well. It was a tough decision, but ultimately I'm glad I decided to stay in Newport, save money and get *Soveraine* exactly the way I wanted her.

I had considered taking the boat to New York; I found a slip for $300 per month right across from lower Manhattan in Jersey City. However, my neighbors would be the Westin and Marriott hotels instead of Newport Shipyard and Casey's Marina. Not conducive to getting boat work done. I'd have to drive a distance to a West Marine and any reputable boat yard. Newport is also cheaper at about $168 per month for dock space, including showers, pool and sauna use!

I was kind of looking forward to it actually. I hadn't spent more than five months in the same place since I left Boston nearly three years ago and was pretty tired of constantly moving. I resolved to get a lot of work on *Soveraine* done as well as a ton of reading and writing.

In mid-October, I took my boat (dinghy hip-tied again) with the help of Geoff to the dock she would re-main at for the next seven months. She was nestled into a corner slip, and my mind started spinning with all that had to be done in these short seven months. It wasn't long before I had the bowsprit off, with the help of the mighty legs of Matt Hartke. I ordered the three, five foot, 2"x6" pieces of teak and had them shipped to Maine with the intent of picking them up at my dad's place up there.

Unfortunately, the Metro wouldn't make it off of Aquidneck Island, which I found out the hard way when it refused to make it over the bridge, and I had to turn around and coast back into Newport. My dad brought them down as he was passing through one week and during a sunny weekend I had them together with some epoxy, cut to shape, sanded and affixed to the stem of *Soveraine*. It sounds easier than it was, but it still wasn't too difficult. Around the same time, Hurricane Sandy came up the eastern seaboard and wreaked some havoc on New York and parts of Connecticut. Rhode Island wasn't hit too hard; we had about a four foot storm surge over the regular high tide. That's part of the beauty of being on a boat for disasters like that, as the water rises so does your floating home, and then lowers when it recedes.

I had also started a job at a desk again. It had been four years since my last 9-5, and I thought I could handle it, especially since I'd be out of there by spring. I was processing mortgages, something completely foreign, but caught on pretty quickly. The schedule was great too; my shift started at three pm and went until 11 since they had a lot of west coast customers. This allowed me to work on my boat while the sun was up and go into work when it got dark.

My dad showed up for Thanksgiving and helped me construct the framing for the shrink wrap that would envelope my boat for the next five months and give me an insulating layer as well as protection from the snow for all the stuff I had laid out on the deck. It went up in a few hours and a couple of days later Green and Mike helped with the shrink wrap. It cost less than $200, which was a blessing.

That December of 2012 marked three years I had been living aboard boats. Reflecting on how far I had come in those three years, as well as a trip to Florida for Christmas reinvigorated my desire and drive to never, ever, spend a winter in New England again. A nor'easter welcomed me back to Newport which was less than inviting to say the least.

The remainder of that winter was spent working at the desk job, coaching a local high school swim team and completing as many projects as I could with the shrink wrap up and still at the dock. One of these was taken away when I tried to go to the desk job one morning in late January. I had parked in a public spot the night before, instead of the private lot, which I sometimes did since it was closer to my boat. When I went out there the next morning, however, my dear blue Metro was nowhere to be found. I went into the Seaman's Church, and they confirmed my suspicions that it had been towed away. I knew exactly why, I had about half a dozen unpaid parking tickets. I called up the towing company, and they gave me the total bill: including the parking tickets, towing, and storage it amounted to over $800. The rest of the conversation went as follows:

Me: You can just keep it then.

Them: What do you mean? You don't want your car?

Me: $800 is worth far more than the value of that thing, keep it.

Them: OK….well, you're going to have to come down and sign off on it.

Me: Where are you guys located?

Them: Down by the rotary.

Me: That's too far to walk, I'm sorry but you towed it away, this is your problem now. Goodbye.

I called my boss as the desk job and told her I'd have to find another way to work and she informed me that I was being laid off. This was a relief actually; I was pulling my hair out at that place and I would be able to get unemployment for a few months before returning to work on *Weatherly* in the spring.

I was also coaching high school swimming, which

was more enjoying than I had thought it would be. There were 18 wonderful student-athletes, and it made me realize that I hadn't really interacted with high school kids since, well, high school. Challenging at times, they were a joy to work with, and I ended up learning a lot about myself as well by the end of the season. Most importantly I started to think that once this next sailing season was over, I might try my hand in education.

Not heading south at the end of the summer had allowed me to get closer to a new, old friend: Elizabeth. I had called her the day after I hit the docks in Newport coming from Bermuda and the disengagement. We had been seeing each other on and off since the summer, but more so over that winter. She was very supportive and knew how much getting this boat ready to go by August meant to me. She had her own thing going too and changed jobs from the firm we worked at together in Boston to another in New York. We had both grown and matured a lot since we had dated last and had a very comfortable relationship developing, one free of expectations since we both knew each other so well by this point.

Late in February I tackled the transmission. It took me the better part of two days to get it out, and not without more than a helping hand from Green. I really don't know where I'd be without that guy's help and advice. I even had to get the engine up off the mounting pads and shuffle it forward to get the gearbox out. I gave it to a guy John Whitney, an old salt who was the resident authority on small diesels (and larger ones too).

He called me a few days later and told me the reason it was stuck in forward was a simple issue of a bolt that had backed itself out! What amazing good luck! He said the rest of the gearbox looked fine, and it would only be $250 for his time. I had it back in the following week, and it only took me about 6 hours to get it back together. I fired her up and, after a few cable adjustments, had it shifting with ease.

I tore into the head as one of my smaller projects and repainted the whole thing as well as refinished the cabinets and installed what I believe is the first legitimate holding tank on the boat in her life. I also rewired and changed the running lights and cabin lights to LED bulbs.

By mid-April, I had the shrink wrap off and that same day Green took Elizabeth and I for a first sail of the season aboard *Lyra*. The first charter on *Weatherly* came early, the last week in April. Sailing season in Newport had officially begun, and the only project I had left to do before I went back to the anchorage was the chainplates.

I had first noticed the funny brown water weeping from the bulkhead, late in the previous summer after some torrential rain. I knew that my chainplates were under there; either the factory or someone else had decided to fiberglass *over* the chainplates attached to the bulkhead (for the masthead shroud) and the ones attached to knees (for the lower shrouds). I also had no idea of the condition of the knees or bulkhead themselves or even what they were made of. I had seen other Seawinds with external chainplates attached to the hull and after talking some design issues over with Ben I decided on external ones, attached to the hull itself, would be the way to go.

I ordered quarter inch bronze plate (I would have preferred three-sixteenths, but that was impossible to find) and had it cut into six chainplates and six backing plates. I then bent them to the shape of my hull and had 46 holes drilled and 20 bronze bolts ordered. Installing them took a few days of careful measuring, drilling, redrilling, etc. and one by one I transferred the turnbuckles and shrouds from the internal to external chainplates. I then cut off the ones sticking up from the deck, leaving them attached inside and epoxied over to seal them off. Now, with all of my dock-necessary projects complete, it was time to head out to the anchorage for another Newport summer.

New chainplates on the hull

XVI
Summer in Newport, Take Three

"I really don't know why it is that all of us are so committed to the sea, except I think it's because in addition to the fact that the sea changes, and the light changes, and ships change, it's because we all came from the sea. And it is an interesting biological fact that all of us have in our veins the exact same percentage of salt in our blood that exists in the ocean, and, therefore, we have salt in our blood, in our sweat, in our tears. We are tied to the ocean. And when we go back to the sea - whether it is to sail or to watch it - we are going back from whence we came."

- John F. Kennedy, Remarks at the Dinner for the America's Cup Crews of *Weatherly* and *Gretel*, September 14, 1962

I was off the dock and back out on the hook by mid-May. Memorial Day was the first time I had her out, and with six people on board she was a full boat! It all went swimmingly until it was time to head back to the anchorage. We doused sail and were motoring from the shipyard back to the anchorage when the engine unexpectedly shut down. I couldn't immediately get her going again so the jib was pulled out and we sailed to a mooring, just missing being impaled on the bowsprit of the mighty sloop *Providence*. Special thanks to Micah,

Gretchen, Seabass, Elizabeth and Liz for the quick hands!

Elizabeth and I on Soveraine, *Narragansett Bay*

I traced it back to a fuel issue; the issue finally being that I didn't have enough fuel in the tank. In my small 11 gallon tank the pickup tube sat so high a solid gallon was left out of reach, something I couldn't have known without actually running out of fuel. No worries, I just marked the tank and kept a mental note for the future. After bleeding the fuel pump and injectors, I was back in business.

Sailing on *Weatherly* was going great. It was wonderful to be back on the water again regularly, especially with such a great owner/captain as George and new crew Rogan. The rain however was putting a damper on sailing for both *Weatherly* as well as *Soveraine*. Out of the first 15 days of June in 2013 it rained for about 13 of them. I tried to not let it get to me, but I was really hoping for a solid summer after the brutal winter we had just been through.

It didn't really warm up until July, which is when *Soveraine* was scheduled for a haulout. On the list of things to do was to install an outboard on the transom as a kind of insurance if the inboard shit the bed on the way south. In addition, she needed paint on her bottom, topsides and a new bootstripe as well as get the head discharge through-hull operational again. The haulout happened to correspond with the hottest week of the summer with temperatures near or slightly above 100. It was tough going, sunup to sundown, scraping (a 5 gallon bucket-full of hard growth), sanding, painting, trying to design an outboard bracket (that Green pointed out would be underwater on a port tack, which trashed that idea), and wrestling a through-hull open. The rudder came off, and the play in the pintles and gudgeons was shored up. All-in-all it took me about six full days, and I was back at the anchorage within a week. The topsides were looking great, and I had chosen a $40/gallon industrial one-part polyurethane paint instead of the $100/gallon "marine" version of the same paint. I was pleased.

In the first week of August, *Weatherly* departed Newport heading for the Vineyard and Nantucket for some racing. I had learned much in the year since the last trip there and was ready for more responsibility. Tom and Blythe were back as well, it was great to be sailing with them again. They had to leave prior to Nantucket though, which meant Rogan and I would be responsible for all actions on the foredeck. We justified our pay though, with an amazing come from behind win over *Columbia* in the last race of the series to take second overall. Elizabeth joined the crew for the Opera House Cup, the parade of wooden boats in Nantucket, as well as the delivery back to Newport.

Haulout, July 2013

XVII
Departing Newport Once Again

"We do not ask a tame seagull why she feels the need to disappear from time to time toward the open sea. She goes, that's all, and it is as simple as a sunbeam, as normal as the blue sky."
- Bernard Moitessier

Soveraine was ready to go. We arrived back from Nantucket on a Monday night and on Tuesday morning I met Chris, a friend of fellow 12 meter sailor Jocy who came up from South Carolina to help me sail south. On Wednesday, we departed for Block Island with absolutely zero breeze in the late August heat. Within five hours, the hook was dropped in the Great Salt Pond where we spent the next two nights waiting for the southwesterly breeze to die and the fresh northerly one to take its place. On Friday morning, we weighed anchor and set out for Cape May. The breeze was a gentle 5-10 knots until completely dying at noon, the sails came down and the motor pushed us along until it filled in, this time from the northeast, at around sunset.

During that afternoon, I witnessed something I hadn't seen before at sea. What started as one or two small flies buzzing around the boat had turned into what seemed like at least three dozen, of all varieties, as well as a couple of flying ants and wasps. We ransacked the cabin looking for a source but found none. The only explanation I could think of was they were being blown off the land and were using us as their life raft, that is, until they met their fate with a rolled up magazine.

Later that night the breeze continued to build and clock around to the east-northeast. By morning, we were running with a gusty 15 knot breeze and a four foot sea under jib and jigger and a cloudless sky, more or less ideal. Dolphins on the bow (and one running into the keel with a distinct thud) and sea turtle sightings rounded out a great day of sailing. By seven that night, the wind died again, and we motored the remaining 50 miles to Cape May, having to kill time outside of the harbor inlet to wait for the sun to rise. We anchored next to the Coast Guard training base at 7 that morning. Thinking back to three years ago, it had taken John and I over 12 days, and two new(er) sails to get this far. It had only taken Chris and I half that time.

Soveraine *at anchor, Cape May, NJ*

***

What a nightmare, I thought to myself in that state of half-awake/half-asleep before even opening my eyes. My dream consisted of a trip to the ER and a diagnosis of a broken heel, which would have certainly put a damper on plans for heading south. But wait, why does my left foot feel tight and constrained? I cracked my left eye open, and an unfamiliar ceiling lay above me. Tilting my head up and gazing down at a mass of cotton and Ace bandages confirmed reality.

The plan was to head south to Norfolk on Wednesday morning, two days after arriving in Cape May. On Monday night Chris and I went out for dinner and went out for some beers after. We met a couple of ladies who convinced us to go swimming at a hotel pool a couple of blocks down. We hopped the gate and I immediately cannon-balled in. Within seconds a security guard was at that gate, blocking the only exit. I hopped out of the pool and ran to a four foot high wall and jumped over, assuming it would be four feet to the street on the other side. A seven foot drop to the sidewalk below was what awaited me. When I tried to get up, I couldn't support my own weight. Some hours later, the ER doctor told me I had broken my heel. I took a taxi back to the dock where Chris was supposed to meet me with the dinghy, but his phone was on silent, so I asked the driver to take me to a cheap hotel. He ended up taking me to Wildwood, a bizarre grid of cheap motels spilling over from Atlantic City.

When I got back to Cape May the next afternoon, I asked about how much it would be to dock my boat there for a month or two while I healed up. The woman behind the counter said they only had a day rate, nothing monthly, and that it would come out to about $1500 for 30 days. She said this with a straight face and a tone that implied $3000 for two months was a reasonable price. New Effin Jersey; that's all I'm going to say. I walked out dumbfounded, and a little scared. Where was I going to put the boat while I was banged up? I immediately put a post to a cruising forum asking if there was any reasonable dockage within the Delaware Bay area. I got a response within the hour that there was a dock in Baltimore for $470/month. Much better. A few minutes later, I then got another message from the same user saying he had just found out his friend was leasing theirs for $125/month, perfect!

We left the next morning, motoring up the Delaware Bay and anchored in the C&D canal basin at about nine that night. I had my splint/bandages wrapped in a plastic bag as it poured rain off and on all day, sitting at the helm in my foul weather jacket and board shorts, hood up and covering my face. Another nine hours of motoring the next day got us into Baltimore at about four in the afternoon. Chris and I buttoned up the boat, and Elizabeth picked me up that night. I spent some time with her family in Arlington, VA and went with her to Hoboken, NJ for a while followed by Sarasota with my mom.

After exactly eight weeks to the day, I was back in Baltimore and ready to continue the trip south. *Soveraine* looked as good (if not better thanks to the rain and not dragging up mud with the anchor) as when I had left, thanks to Chris for putting her to bed so well.

Not a moment too soon either, the temperature had dropped considerably and was supposed to be in the upper 30s when we started down the Chesapeake. A 12 meter friend Zach arrived the day before our departure and was promptly pick-pocketed in the Baltimore train station. What a welcome. A spry 19 year old Pearce rounded out our crew for heading down to Norfolk.

It was cold leaving Baltimore. Damn cold. Mid-40s during the day and low 30s at night. The winds were right though and within an hour of leaving the dock the sails were up and we were going at a good clip in the northwesterly breeze. It really picked up during the day and lasted into the night. It felt really good to be sailing *Soveraine* again, even if it was bitterly cold with the wind that night. We motored into Norfolk the next day and slid into a slip at the public, i.e. free, docks in Portsmouth.

We were putting the boat away when a troop of three people about my age came down to the boat.

"What kind of boat is she?"

"Allied Seawind."

"Oh nice! My wife and I were looking at those. We ended up buying a Hans Christian 38."

I invited the three of them onboard and after a few beers the conversation drifted to where we had all been, and I mentioned my previous trip down the ICW that ended in Beaufort three years ago. One of the women (not in the married couple) looked surprised and said she too was in Beaufort at that time, living on a boat. I looked back at her, and it struck me.

"Were you living with your boyfriend on a Grampian 26?" I asked.

"Yes..."

"And were you working at a coffee and wine bar?"

"...yes..."

"Lindsay, its Scott! I've met both you and Jay before!"

We stared back at each other for a few seconds before those around us started commenting on how serendipitous and bizarre this whole thing was. We all went out in Norfolk together that night and did what cruisers do when they meet other cruisers: talk about cruising.

Zach was with us for the next two days, motoring through Coinjock and down to my fellow *Weatherly* crew Rogan's place on Roanoke Island. Rogan cooked us shepherd's pie which was one of the best meals I've ever had, especially considering this was coming off a night of Spam, and instant mashed potatoes (now a staple on *Soveraine*, thank you Chris). Pearce and I took her the rest of the way to Beaufort, motoring across a sunny and eerily calm Pamlico Sound, arriving on Halloween. It was pretty strange being back there (three years exactly), but not a lot had changed, which was a relief.

The forecast for leaving Beaufort was getting more menacing with each update. Initially, it was calling for 15-20 knots, gusting to 25 out of the northeast. It would be at our backs, but the seas would be confused coming right off a strong southwesterly. This would be OK, I thought, they would settle out before we got too far from shore, or we could hug the coast. Tony, a friend from Newport, thought otherwise and suggested we go inside. He said it was one of the better parts of the ICW, and he was right. Saturday morning solidified those plans when the forecast was upgraded to winds gusting to 30 knots. I may have attempted it with a more experienced crew but with just Pearce I was basically single handing, at best. No offence to Pearce, he's enthusiastic and a quick learner, but throwing him, myself and this boat in the deep end that quickly is not something I'm willing to do. We left Beaufort at dawn a few days after Halloween to motor down the ICW to Charleston. I checked the oil dipstick and to my delight it was not white nor the consistency of butter.

It took us four and a half days to get from Beaufort to Charleston, all motoring along the ICW. The highlights were the breathtaking scenery along the Waccamaw River in South Carolina and doing nine knots over the bottom in the Cape Fear River, with the help of a two and a half knot current and motor sailing downwind with gusts to 30 knots at our backs. In Georgetown, I came across some boats with torn sails that had left Beaufort the night before we did and tried to brave those conditions offshore. I was sure glad we took the more conservative route.

Arriving in Charleston, we were greeted by one of the best hostesses a city could ever ask for, a friend I met there a few months ago, Anita. She met us at the dock, her former place of employment, with mimosas in hand and spent the rest of the day touring the city with us. The following day a larger ketch pulled in and the captain was none other than my friend Drew, a guy I met on my first delivery on *When and If*! And as it turned out Hugh, another guy I met on that same delivery was living in Charleston! I hadn't seen these guys in over three years, and it was wonderful reminiscing and catching up with them. On our last night in town (Drew and I had both decided to depart Charleston on the same day) Anita hosted all of us, as well as her three friends, for a spectacular dinner party.

Pearce and I were up at sunrise the next morning but couldn't get off the dock due to current issues; it rips through the marina at almost 3 knots. We waited for slack tide at noon and were off. It was a beautiful sunny day, and the wind was about 10 knots out of the northeast, which built throughout the afternoon. I'm usually pretty good about seasickness but I won't lie, on this day I wasn't. The seas were a very moderate three to five feet, but something hit me the wrong way, and I spent the next 18 hours in agony. I think it may have been the head cold I had, messing with my inner ear equilibrium and amplifying and feeling of uneasiness. I was pretty much over it by the next morning though, but the wind had died and then switched to the southwest, so we motor sailed the remainder of the way into Fernandina Beach. It was surreal coming into St. Mary's inlet, with Florida to port and Georgia to starboard. I had done it. After four years the goal I had set for myself was finally coming to fruition and at 10 pm, 34 hours after leaving Charleston, with my anchor resting on a sandy Florida bottom, it had.

XVIII
Finally Florida

"A sailor's joys are as simple as a child's." - Bernard Moitessier

Fernandina Beach is an interesting place. It has a cute, quaint downtown area with more bars per square mile than Newport, which is definitely saying something. A few days after I arrived, my good sailing friend Joey joined me, and we spent the next few nights reveling in the small town and waiting for the weather to change. A cold front had stalled out over the eastern Florida coast and was not making an easy decision as to when to leave. After a few days, we kinda just said to Hell with it and proceeded down the ICW at about four pm on a Thursday.

I didn't think motoring down the ICW at night would be a huge deal, I had done it before, but in this case it turns out I was wrong. Thankfully nothing dreadful happened, but when a day marker that's neither on your Navionics app, nor your paper charts, appears out of the pitch black darkness a mere 15 feet to starboard, it's a freaky experience. I'd done this in twilight before, in a much wider waterway with many well-lit buoys; the narrow, dark channel between Fernandina and the St. Johns River was a different story. Oh yeah, and throw in a huge dredger who we had trouble getting in contact with just for kicks. Joey and I decided to anchor, but not without running aground coming into the anchorage (I blame the Navionics app, it switched from a color-coded chart with numbers marking the depth to a unitless contour map) and spending the better part of an hour trying to kedge ourselves off.

We motored down the St. Johns River the next morning, heading into the open Atlantic. The NOAA buoys still said there was a 7.5 ft sea and winds out of the northeast gusting to 20 knots. Neither was accurate. There was still a five to six foot swell from the east but zero breeze. Sigh...this would be a long 48 hours, and indeed it was. We motored the whole 210 miles down the eastern coast of Florida in little to no breeze for 47 straight hours. We did sail a little on the final morning when it finally picked up again out of the north.

One thing I've discovered about myself is that I am not a sailing purist. I used to think I might be, reading books by the Pardey's, Moitessier, and other engineless sailors; but that's just not my bag. Sailing is a lifestyle and sport that demands patience as it is, even under the best conditions I'm only going about seven miles per hour. If the wind isn't blowing in my favor, or at all, I'll admit I'm quick to turn on the "iron spinnaker" and just get somewhere. I really don't mind it either, for me voyaging is more about the experience of travel and discovery than bobbing about in a windless ocean for days at a time.

After spending a week and a half over Thanksgiving at my brother's place in Stuart, it was time to weigh anchor and head over to the west coast. I had a great time in Stuart, seeing family, resting and even met up with Scott and Kitty again which is always a pleasure. Stuart was not my final destination though, and I was starting to wonder if I even had one.

I was getting desperate for some other crew and wanted to leave by the end of the week when a guy named Chris responded to my ad on a cruising forum. I had sailed with people from that forum before; it was how I got in touch with Alex and got on the whole Hawaii/Alaska/San Diego expedition. Two days later he flew into West Palm, and we left the following morning.

I decided to take the Okeechobee Waterway across the state as opposed to going around the tip of Florida and through the Keys. I've heard with the Gulf Stream so close to the reefs it can get a little intimidating trying to shoot between them. It only took us two days to get from Stuart to Ft Myers, with some great sailing on Lake Okeechobee. We also traveled through five locks, two on the east side of the lake to bring *Soveraine* up to the level of the lake and three on the west side to lower her back to sea level. Most locks use valves to raise or lower the water level, but on these five locks they simply open the gates! It can be a shock the first time you see it, but it was pretty neat and very simple.

We spent the first night in Clewiston Rock City, at a dock that I was pressured into getting, when I called to simply find the rate for the night. The guy at the marina called me all afternoon, assuring me he'd be there to show me where to go and tie me up, he kept saying his name was Little Man or something, odd and demeaning nonetheless. After navigating the narrow channel in total darkness, with Chris on the bow with a spotlight, I gave Little Man a call and he said he'd left for the night. I was kind of ticked off since he had repeatedly told me he would wait, but he gave me another number to call, which didn't work. We found the dock, tied up, and told ourselves that we would be out of there before dawn to give them the slip for such lousy service. Our plans were thwarted however when we met an Irish guy, totally out of place in Clewiston, who bought us round after round of Jameson shots. I forgot to set my alarm and woke up with Little Man standing right at the boat. We were in Ft Myers the next night, after a thankfully uneventful motor the rest of the way across the state.

I saw Alaina when we got to Ft. Myers for the first time in a year and half, she was living back in her hometown. Things went well, considering the past, and I saw her as nothing more than a friend. I invited her to sail with us the next day to Sarasota, which I didn't think she would take me up on, but she did.

We were off the mooring early afternoon the next day and promptly ran aground south of Lofton's Island in a spot that was not clearly marked on the chart. We could have waited until the tide came up at six that night, but I wanted to get going so TowBoatUS came to the rescue. Underway again, we cleared out of San Carlos Bay around sunset and motored on a glassy Gulf of Mexico into the night around Sanibel and Captiva. The wind picked up on my watch around two in the morning, and I set the sails myself, not wanting to wake my crewmates. I turned the engine off, and

Soveraine slid over the light chop at five knots with a gentle easterly land breeze. This was, more or less, the moment I had been working towards for over a year and a half restoring the 50 year old Allied Seawind, with a little twist of irony that Alaina was sleeping below on the boat I purchased with her former engagement ring as I completed the trip home to Sarasota. I'd that's pretty much full circle.

The sails came down at dawn, and the engine pushed us between the Venice jetties as we motored up the ICW to Sarasota. Just before noon, Chris grabbed a mooring pennant in the bay that I had fought against being installed two years earlier, another small ironic situation. We took the dinghy ashore and walked up Main Street, back in my hometown.

Epilogue

After arriving in Florida, the plan was to keep sailing for a bit. Down through the Keys and over to the Bahamas most likely, but I couldn't find willing crew. I had lived alone on a boat for most of the prior five years, and decided to move in with (and get engaged to) Elizabeth up in New Jersey.

Soveraine is at a dock near Mom's place in the Tampa Bay area and I visit every few months. She'll remain there for the next few years as I start a new career in education and refill the cruising kitty. In addition, I want to make her ocean-ready before I set out on the next adventure. This includes a wind vane self-steering system, replacing the standing rigging, new (or at least newer) sails, and a life raft to name a few.

In the end, I wouldn't have done a thing differently. I still consider leaving the engineering desk job in Boston to be one of the best decisions I've ever made. The past few years as my introduction to the cruising world has set the stage for a lifetime of adventure, and for that I am truly grateful. Having my own cruising boat and the knowledge to sail it is the ace up my sleeve; no matter what happens outside of my little sailing world I've built for myself, I can always come back to it and nobody can ever take that away.

Made in the USA
Charleston, SC
02 October 2014